Media and Management

IN SEARCH OF MEDIA

Timon Beyes, Mercedes Bunz, and Wendy Hui Kyong Chun,
Series Editors

Media and Management

**Rutvica Andrijasevic, Julie Yujie Chen,
Melissa Gregg, and Marc Steinberg**

IN SEARCH OF MEDIA

University of Minnesota Press
Minneapolis
London

meson press

In Search of Media is a collaboration between the University
of Minnesota Press and meson press, an open access
publisher, https://meson.press

Published by the University of Minnesota Press, 2021
111 Third Avenue South, Suite 290
Minneapolis, MN 55401-2520
https://www.upress.umn.edu

in collaboration with
meson press
Salzstrasse 1
21335 Lüneburg, Germany
https://meson.press

ISBN 978-1-5179-1224-6 (pb)
Library of Congress record available at
https://lccn.loc.gov/2021028226.

The University of Minnesota is an equal-opportunity educator
and employer.

UMP BmB 2021

Contents

Series Foreword

"Media determine our situation," Friedrich Kittler infamously wrote in his Introduction to *Gramophone, Film, Typewriter.* Although this dictum is certainly extreme—and media archaeology has been critiqued for being overly dramatic and focused on technological developments—it propels us to keep thinking about media as setting the terms for which we live, socialize, communicate, organize, do scholarship, et cetera. After all, as Kittler continued in his opening statement almost thirty years ago, our situation, "in spite or because" of media, "deserves a description." What, then, are the terms—the limits, the conditions, the periods, the relations, the phrases—of media? And, what is the relationship between these terms and determination? This book series, *In Search of Media,* answers these questions by investigating the often elliptical "terms of media" under which users operate. That is, rather than produce a series of explanatory keyword-based texts to describe media practices, the goal is to understand the conditions (the "terms") under which media is produced, as well as the ways in which media impacts and changes these terms.

Clearly, the rise of search engines has fostered the proliferation and predominance of keywords and terms. At the same time, it has changed the very nature of keywords, since now any word and pattern can become "key." Even further, it has transformed the very process of learning, since search presumes that, (a) with the right phrase, any question can be answered and (b) that the answers lie within the database. The truth, in other words, is "in there." The impact of search/media on knowledge, however, goes beyond search engines. Increasingly, disciplines—from sociology to economics, from the arts to literature—are in search of media as a way to revitalize their methods and objects of study. Our current media situation therefore seems to imply a new term, understood as temporal shifts of mediatic conditioning. Most broadly, then, this series asks: What are the terms or conditions of knowledge itself?

To answer this question, each book features interventions by two (or more) authors, whose approach to a term—to begin with: *communication, pattern discrimination, markets, remain, machine, archives, organize, action at a distance, undoing networks*—diverge and converge in surprising ways. By pairing up scholars from North America and Europe, this series also advances media theory by obviating the proverbial "ten year gap" that exists across language barriers due to the vagaries of translation and local academic customs and in order to provoke new descriptions, prescriptions, and hypotheses—to rethink and reimagine what media can and must do.

Introduction

Platform Capitalism Has a Hardware History

Rutvica Andrijasevic, Julie Yujie Chen, Melissa Gregg, and Marc Steinberg

Management's Mediation

Whether it is considered a science, a professional discipline, an operation of control, or a technique of self-enhancement, management is a cultural practice that takes different forms over space and time. This book argues that management is enabled by various forms of media, just as those media give life to management. By media we refer to the large and small objects and technologies that transmit, produce, or encircle the practice of management and its experience by workers. Knowing that management ideas are produced through deliberate techniques of composition, persuasion, and interpellation is an important step toward resisting the commonsense imperatives that govern our lives, whether at work, at home, or in the many worlds between.

Over time, the stopwatch, the punch card, the calculator, and the camera are but a selection of media types that have catalyzed management innovations (Beyes, Holt, and Pias 2019). Theories of management are constantly manufactured and disseminated through printed and virtual textbooks, mass-market self-help paperback guides, TED talks, corporate consulting, and other

motivational genres (Gregg 2018). More recently, sensing and
positioning capabilities embedded in smartphones and watches
have made management all the more intimate, as disciplinary
technologies nudge the mind and body with corrective haptics.
In the age of "platform capitalism" (Srnicek 2016), hardware and
software protocols encourage new governance techniques and
forms of pattern discrimination (Apprich et al. 2018). Workers
are learning to adjust their speed and motions to algorithmically
defined rhythms that are often purposefully designed to remain
elusive (Siciliano 2017). Through each stage of the evolving relationship between workers and employers, producers and consumers,
management is learned and disseminated through media, while
new media formats produce fresh opportunities for subjectification
and control.

It remains novel to examine management from the angle of its
mediations. Building on the authors' complementary backgrounds,
this book provides insight on the changing models of labor composition, performance, and governance that are not only characteristic of present experience but generative of global dependencies.
We pay close attention to the geographies and histories of media
and their complementary coexistence with management.

The title *Media and Management* may suggest our aim is merely
to add media to existing management analysis. However, for us
media are not a qualifier for management, they are how management works. The field of "media management" already deals with
the operation of the media industries in particular. Our concern is
with the interpenetration of media in all aspects of management,
showing how management always manifests through media and
through various mediations. It is this media–management nexus
that the chapters in this volume track in distinct ways: from the use
of "kanban" cards in the Toyota automobile production system, to
the dependence on Facebook for recruiting workers on a just-in-
time basis, to the mediation of government policy and third-party
staffing agencies in app-based food-delivery services. Our basic
claim is that these managerial techniques should be the object of

media studies as much as television or Netflix; conversely, management should be as concerned with media as it is with efficiencies or organizations.

The book charts a different course than research on media and management undertaken in *media industry studies* (also known as "production studies"; see, for example, Caldwell 2008; Deuze 2011; Lotz 2014; Mayer, Banks, and Caldwell 2009), and *media management studies,* represented in journals such as *Journal of Media Business Studies* or *International Journal on Media Management.* These traditions are mainly concerned with the production, distribution, and marketing of media content (television, film, radio, or streaming video) and necessarily circumscribe their analysis to the study of management in the context of professional and pro-amateur practices. In this book we focus on media as a condition of management. In doing so we examine the general mediality that is constitutive of all management operations, with a special attention to the nexus of management and labor.

Media, as a term, can refer to specific forms—newspapers, television, magazines, film, etc.—just as it can mean the condition of mediation in general. W. T. J. Mitchell and Mark Hansen push us to focus on the latter in their *Critical Terms for Media Studies* (2010), wherein they argue that, post-McLuhan, the project of "understanding media" (McLuhan 1994) is studying the effects of media (and mediation) on life itself. They suggest a shift of emphasis from discrete mediums to the "collective singular *media*" (Mitchell and Hansen 2010, viii), which is to say, media as a condition of lived experience.

Weihong Bao (2015, 8) advances the project of understanding media further by distinguishing three conceptual models of the medium:

> (1) a linear model of the medium as a directional transmission of a message (2) an intermediary model that conceives medium as the interface and intervening entity facilitating the two-way exchange between the subject

and the objective world, and (3) a spherical model that understands the medium as an immediate environment or field that encompasses a variety of media and constitutes a shared space of experience.

The *linear* model refers to the classic communication studies definition of media as a means of transmitting a message. In this volume, this occurs when a message is sent via Viber seeking available workers for imminent production orders, or, in the Toyotist production model, when a "kanban" message transfers from one part of the plant to another, asking for more supplies of a given automobile part. The *intermediary* model suggests a more organic connection between medium, message, and social totality. We find this model at work in recent theories of software interface (Chun 2005; Galloway 2012), as well as in platform theory, when the platform itself is conceived as an intermediary between two or more parties entering into a financial transaction. Examples in this book include temporary work agencies that are operating as medium-intermediaries between multiple parties in managing workforces (Andrijasevic and Sacchetto 2017). Finally, the *spherical* model, which posits the medium as environment, recalls Marshall McLuhan's treatment of the medium as message. In this influential view, the message stands for the totality of social transformations effectuated by the introduction of a particular medium. The train is important not for what it carries (its message, in the transmission model) but for the social changes it enacts upon the whole of society. For instance, the settler-colonial nation of Canada (as environment) was constituted via the railway network connecting East to West. In our examples, the factory and the collective worker dormitory are environments for managing workers' cross-border mobility. So too the city is an environment created and traversed by delivery workers, mediated by smartphone apps.

To Bao's linear, intermediary, and spherical models of media we add a fourth: media as organizational force (Beyes et al. 2019; Beyes, Holt, and Pias 2019). Media function as ordering devices, that is, as means of organization—whether for companies or by

political formations. This is particularly relevant to the analysis of
management's mediations. Management relies on media as organizational tools, from time clocks to enterprise resource planning
software to digital platforms. Such tools also work to embody the
means and methods of management itself. The manufacture order
form, popular guidebooks, government policy documents, dormitories, and temporary work agencies are all telling objects of analysis
for the ways management is mediated. As we seek to understand
their force, broader themes emerge: the geopolitical tensions
around management practices, theories of time embedded in
supply chains, and the role of platforms in organizing life and
labor today. Mediation is a valuable point of departure to question
the means by which management exerts control, and the power
relations that are constitutive of and manifested through the linear,
intermediary, spherical, or organizational models of media.

Management's Hardware History

Two concepts guide our engagement with media and management:
"just-in-time" (JIT) and the platform. Both organizational models
illustrate the Asia-Pacific derivations of management practices
throughout history.

Just-In-Time

Traditionally, the concept of just-in-time (JIT) refers to a system of
temporal contraction and inventory management, wherein a good
or service is produced only as it is needed for a subsequent part
of the production process. Coming out of the Toyota Production
System, as Marc Steinberg discusses in chapter 1, JIT is also
closely associated with the temporal dynamics and supply-chain
management of the logistical turn. Expanding on this tradition,
Rutvica Andrijasevic argues that humans, not just automobile parts,
are now the object of JIT management. In chapter 2, she shows
how the temporal contraction of JIT is used in the transnational
management of a temporary migrant workforce supporting Asian-
owned electronics manufacturing and its expansion into Central

and Eastern Europe. On-demand workforce assembly is further discussed by Julie Yujie Chen in chapter 3. Food-delivery labor is shown to be treated as modular and flexible, ready to disassemble and reassemble by platforms as well as temporary staffing agencies in China. In showing the centrality of manufacturing in the development of JIT and on-demand logics, we stress the dependencies between assembly and consumption that remain insufficiently explored in media studies today, despite a renewed interest in the materiality of media (exceptions include Qiu 2017; Qiu, Gregg, and Crawford 2014; Nakamura 2014). Focusing on employment experiences and labor practices that are often neglected as a by-product of consumer convenience in the adoption of digital devices, an emphasis on hardware also expands the horizon of labor geography that otherwise takes the software-centrism of present-day Silicon Valley as given.

Platform

The hardware affordances of platforms have long been a priority for games studies (Montfort and Bogost, 2009). By contrast, communications studies scholars (Gillespie 2010; Poell, Nieborg, and van Dijck 2019) see the platform as a rhetorical device, acting as a strategy to obfuscate ownership (most famously in the case of Facebook) or setting algorithmic controls that determine user experience. Media studies of the past decade tended to treat platforms first and foremost as discrete software or hardware phenomena (such as YouTube or the Atari game system), only subsequently acknowledging the crucial role managerial ideas play in the platform's formation. In the business world, a separate line of thought regarded the platform as an intermediary enabling economic transactions between multiple parties (Kokuryō 1994; Rochet and Tirole 2003; Steinberg 2019; Athique 2019). In this model, the platform owner manages each side of the transaction: revenue accrues by influencing the terms of connection and mediation between individuals, goods, and services. As this model of innovation spans to include software as much as hardware (eBay, Alibaba, and Google

all count as platforms in this vision), we see ongoing reconfigura-
tion of the terms of participation, competition, collaboration, distribution, and value creation in the modern economy, reorganizing
both platform users and laborers (Gawer 2011; Kenney and Zysman 2016). Reflecting on these rich lineages of platform thinking
is to see the platform first and foremost as a managerial concept,
steeped in a history of hardware manufacture, and deeply tied to
changing efforts of extracting labor and profit.

As authors we share an interest in looking beyond the contemporary digital era for the history, practice, and theory of the platform
economy (Chen 2020). It is clear that Toyotism in Japan gave rise
to foundational skills, products, workplace environments, and
just-in-time principles that informed the transition from analogue
to digital capitalism. Toyotism typically marks the beginning of
competitive tension between the United States and Japanese
business culture. In the mid-twentieth century so-called bottom-up
efficiency measures were seen to enhance factory output and
quality. In the 1970s and '80s, corporations such as Sony and Nin-
tendo inherited these dynamics as mass-market media ecologies
and new consumer devices took shape. These in turn become the
basis for platform business models epitomized by Japan's i-mode
mobile Internet service. I-mode created a formula for subsequent
platformization adopted by U.S. companies like Apple and Google,
even if this history is not widely known (Steinberg 2019).

For media studies to accurately reflect the management of digital
labor therefore requires shifting attention from Silicon Valley to the
powerful force of the Asia Pacific. Global geographies of production
are the legacy of hardware and manufacturing companies and
their accompanying management methods. It is the trans-Pacific
encounter between the United States and Japan that produced
the concept of "lean manufacture" that now bleeds into software
design, start-up mantras, and efficiency methods in the present,
as Marc Steinberg explains. Likewise, it is contemporary Asian
manufacturing companies that influence how intra-European
manufacturing geographies are formed, managed, and displayed—

through the cross-border staffing industry and European Union legal apparatus of "posted workers" outlined by Rutvica Andrijasevic. Even more recently, it is government policies behind China's "new economy" that give rise to images of on-demand workers as entrepreneurial heroes in a pandemic, in the writing of Julie Yujie Chen.

The terms of media and management outlined in this book are perhaps no better realized than in the story of Japan's SoftBank. Founded by Korean-Japanese Masayoshi Son, SoftBank started as a software sales network in 1981, invested in Yahoo in 1995, launched Yahoo Japan as a joint venture in 1996 (which to this day remains one of the top three most-visited sites in Japan), and made an early, large investment in Alibaba. In the 2000s, SoftBank bought or built telecommunications companies in Japan (Yahoo BB broadband internet in 2001 and SoftBank mobile in 2006) and the United States (Sprint in 2013), acquired U.K.-based chip maker ARM in 2016 and reached an agreement to sell it to NVIDIA in 2020, and merged its Yahoo Japan subsidiary with tech and social media giant LINE in 2021 (Tanaka 2019). Leveraging his success as an early investor in U.S. and Chinese tech "unicorns," Son evolved SoftBank from a tech and telecommunications emphasis on the first part of its portmanteau—Soft(ware)—to the second part of its portmanteau, Bank. With its $100 billion USD "Vision Fund" SoftBank aimed to become a finance platform that would disrupt the financiers of the disrupters, taking on Silicon Valley's boutique venture capital world, and extending to worldwide real estate (Wiedeman 2020).

From communications hardware to social media sites, silicon chips to leasing property, SoftBank's ascendency encapsulates the opportunity and unaccountability of financial markets that ultimately underwrite platform economics. SoftBank's recent joint venture with Toyota in ride hailing and food delivery (Nussey and Tajitsu 2019) brings this book full circle, as app developers and telco operators become the future of the automobile industry. Software histories are also hardware futures. In an era when "services define software, and software defines hardware" (Tanaka 2019, 11) the merger between SoftBank subsidiary and LINE and the joint venture with Toyota points to a future where automobiles are, once again, the drivers of the platform economy. Lean manufacture and just-in-time mutate from manufacturing principles to the governing logic of app-mediated, on-demand delivery services. In this, automobile and smartphone converge as the most celebrated forms of mobility, and the boundaries between factory manufacture and platform mediation seem to blur. It is increasingly difficult to determine who is a worker or a manager when we are all, in fact, the product.

As part of the larger *In Search of Media* series, the case studies and interdisciplinary approaches contained here provoke reflection on the power dynamics behind dominant frameworks in media and management studies alike. The car factory and the smartphone share an inheritance, namely, the engineering of efficiency that has always been the goal of managerial oversight. By introducing the topic and practice of management as a key term for the field of media studies, we hope to consolidate the growing community of scholars working at the crossroads of media theory, philosophy, labor, business, and organization studies. Never forgetting the complex "assembly lines" that produce the tools of our own labor, we share these chapters to inspire further collaborations between cultures, disciplines, and working locations that are necessarily entangled in, but never wholly subject to management mandates.

References

Andrijasevic, Rutvica, and Devi Sacchetto. 2017. "'Disappearing Workers': Foxconn in Europe and the Changing Role of Temporary Work Agencies." *Work, Employment and Society* 31, no. 1: 54–70.

Apprich, Clemens, Wendy Hui Kyong Chun, Florian Cramer, and Hito Steyerl. 2018. *Pattern Discrimination.* Minneapolis: University of Minnesota Press and meson press.

Athique, Adrian. 2019 "Digital Emporiums: Platform Capitalism in India." *Media Industries Journal* 6, no. 2. https://doi.org/10.3998/mij.15031809.0006.205.

Bao, Weihong. 2015. *Fiery Cinema: The Emergence of an Affective Medium in China, 1915–1945.* Minneapolis: University of Minnesota Press.

Beyes, Timon, Lisa Conrad, Geert Lovink, Reinhold Martin, and Ned Rossiter. 2019. *Organize*. Minneapolis: University of Minnesota Press and meson press.

Beyes, Timon, Robin Holt, and Claus Pias. 2019. *The Oxford Handbook of Media, Technology, and Organization Studies*. Oxford: Oxford University Press.

Caldwell, John Thornton. 2008. *Production Culture: Industrial Reflexivity and Critical Practice in Film and Television*. Durham, N.C.: Duke University Press.

Chen, Julie Yujie. 2020. "The Mirage and Politics of Participation in China's Platform Economy." *Javnost—The Public* 27, no. 2: 154–70. https://doi.org/10.1080/13183222 .2020.1727271.

Chun, Wendy Hui Kyong. 2005. "On Software, or the Persistence of Visual Knowledge." *Grey Room* 18 (Winter): 26–51.

Deuze, Mark. 2011. *Managing Media Work*. Thousand Oaks, Calif: Sage.

Galloway, Alexander. 2012. *The Interface Effect*. Malden, Mass.: Polity.

Gawer, Annabelle, ed. 2011. *Platforms, Markets, and Innovation*. Cheltenham, UK: Edward Elgar Publishers.

Gillespie, Tarleton. 2010. "The Politics of 'Platforms.'" *New Media & Society* 12, no. 3: 347–64.

Gregg, Melissa. 2018. *Counterproductive: A Brief History of Time Management*. Durham, N.C.: Duke University Press.

Kenney, Martin, and John Zysman. 2016. "The Rise of the Platform Economy." *Issues in Science and Technology,* Spring. http://issues.org/32-3/the-rise-of-the-platform -economy/.

Kokuryō, J. 1994. "Purattofōmu Bijinesu No Torihiki Chūkai Kinō to 'Ōpun-Kei Keiei'" (Platform businesses as facilitators of transactions and their role in encouraging 'open' management). In *Purattofōmu Bijinesu* (Platform business), ed. Imai K. and Kokuryō J., special issue of *InfoCom REVIEW* (Winter 1994): 12–20.

Lotz, Amanda. 2014. "Building Theories of Creative Industry Managers." In *Making Media Work: Cultures of Management in the Entertainment Industries,* ed. Derek Johnson, Derek Kompare, and Avi Santo, 25–38. New York: New York University Press.

Mayer, Vicki, Miranda J. Banks, and John T. Caldwell. 2009. *Production Studies: Cultural Studies of Media Industries*. Oxfordshire, U.K.: Routledge.

McLuhan, Marshall. 1994. *Understanding Media: The Extensions of Man*. Cambridge, Mass.: MIT Press.

Mitchell, William John Thomas, and Mark B. N. Hansen, ed. 2010. *Critical Terms for Media Studies*. Chicago: University of Chicago Press.

Montfort, Nick, and Ian Bogost. 2009. *Racing the Beam: The Atari Video Computer System*. Cambridge, Mass.: MIT Press.

Nakamura, Lisa. 2014. "Indigenous Circuits: Navajo Women and the Racialization of Early Electronic Manufacture." *American Quarterly* 66, no. 4: 919–41.

Nussey, Sam, and Naomi Tajitsu. 2019. "First Stop Southeast Asia: SoftBank, Toyota's Autonomous Car Venture Heads Overseas." *Reuters,* June 11, 2019; https://fr .reuters.com/article/us-softbank-toyota-monet-autonomous-idUSKCN1TC0ZK.

Poell, T., D. Nieborg, D., and J. van Dijck. 2019. "Platformisation." *Internet Policy Review* 8, no. 4. DOI: 10.14763/2019.4.1425.

Qiu, Jack Linchuan. 2017. *Goodbye iSlave: A Manifesto for Digital Abolition.* Champaign: University of Illinois Press.

Qiu, Jack Linchuan, Melissa Gregg, and Kate Crawford. 2014. "Circuits of Labour: A Labour Theory of the iPhone Era." *TripleC: Communication, Capitalism & Critique. Open Access Journal for a Global Sustainable Information Society* 12, no. 2: 564–81.

Rochet, J. C., and J. Tirole. 2003. "Platform Competition in Two-Sided Markets." *Journal of the European Economic Association* 1, no. 4: 990–1029.

Siciliano, Michael. 2017. "Digital Labor's Blackboxed Supervisors." *New Criticals.* October 16, 2017; http://www.newcriticals.com/digital-labors-blackboxed-supervisors.

Srnicek, N. 2016. *Platform Capitalism.* Malden, Mass.: Polity.

Steinberg, Marc. 2019. *The Platform Economy: How Japan Transformed the Comsumer Internet.* Minneapolis: University of Minnesota Press.

Tanaka, Michiaki. 2019. *Sofuto Banku de Uranau 2025 Nen No Sekai* (Predicting the world in 2025 through SoftBank). Tokyo: PHP Business Shinsho.

Wiedeman, Reeves. 2020. *Billion Dollar Loser: The Epic Rise and Spectacular Fall of Adam Neumann and WeWork.* New York: Little, Brown and Company.

Management's Mediations: The Case of Toyotism

Marc Steinberg

From megaphones to timecards, cameras to software, management is always mediated. It relies on various means and modes of transmission abetted by the technical systems of the day, whether 16mm film in early industrial PR (Wasson 2021) to today's YouTube videos, and on manuals, self-help books, newspaper articles, and TED talks. Management inevitably involves mediations and media. This chapter focuses on the mediations of the Toyota Production System and the material medium of the *kanban* card in organizing this system. Reflecting the mandate of this book, this chapter is concerned not with the management *of* mass media but the granular manner in which management operates through media.

It does so by parsing three aspects of management's mediation. First, the *mediation of managerial practice.* This refers to the devices, media objects, and physical means for the execution of managerial aims. Within the sociotechnical assemblage of the factory and the assembly line, for instance, the clock, the time punch card, the organization of space in the factory, communicational media from paper to computer screens dictating production schedules—all of these constitute the media of management. They are what some have called "gray media" (Conrad 2019; Fuller and Goffey 2012) as distinct from the mass media that most often is the focus of media studies. We can think of these as the tools, mediums, and milieus by which management is enacted, drawing on an organizational model of media (Beyes, Conrad, and Martin 2019), which emphasizes the ways in which media function as ordering devices.

Second, this chapter attends to *management's mediatization.* This refers to the circulation of management ideas via particular media forms, such as books, newspapers, or corporate manuals. This second aspect foregrounds the ways that management ideas or paradigms are systematized and packaged with an eye to their transmission to other people, other locations, and other organizations. These people could include other managers within an organization, in which case this is the passing on of managerial doctrine through written means. This could also be through the various genres of management literature, from airport bestsellers through semi-academic books on to more academic studies of management practices. These management books transmit and mediate ideas about managerial practices, operate as self-help literature for the managerial class (Gregg 2018), and, in turn, construct ideas about capitalism, the economy, office work, factories, and labor.

In a third moment, the mediatization of management works back into management practices under transformed conditions. I call this *management's mobilization.* This mobilization sees knowledge created about management in one realm transposed into another—from automobile manufacture to software development, and from Japan to the United States.

This chapter is organized around tracking these developments. Management is operationalized through media (mediation of management). Media are the vehicles and sites whereby management ideas and practices become public and circulate (mediatization of management). The representations of management practices then work back into the workplace habits and practices (management's mobilization). Mediation, mediatization, and mobilization are three moments in a circular process by which management is effected, transmitted, and operationalized (Figure 1).

This chapter tracks these three moments in relation to the managerial practices, representations, and mobilizations of the Toyota Production System (TPS) or "Toyotism," particularly during the 1980s and 1990s. In so doing it attends to how management thought and practices are mediated by particular media systems and geographies.[1] Toyotism designates a set of production practices based on the innovations of Japanese auto manufacturer Toyota from the 1950s onward, including a particularly low-tech means of information transmission known as the *kanban* system. In a wider sense Toyotism designates a shift in manufacturing, a variant on "post-Fordism" as a new logic of manufacture and industry that includes small-batch production and ideas of worker autonomy (Tomaney 1994). Toyotism was the focal point of American and

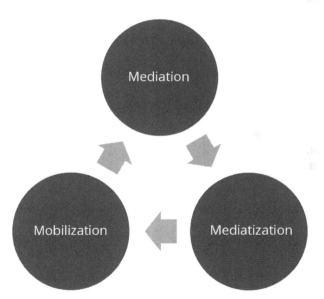

[Figure 1.1]. The three moments of management's mediation.

European auto analysts and management writers whose work promised a view into what was framed as the future of manufacture. Toyotism was also a site of intense geopolitical anxieties over shifts in manufacturing practice and Japan's industrial and economic dominance that came to a head in the 1980s. At this moment in Europe and the United States there was an increasing panic around Japan overtaking Western countries, resulting in the racist discourse known as "Japan-bashing" (Miyoshi 1991; Morris 2013), which is a preview to the anti-Chinese rhetoric prevalent in many countries today.

Focusing on Toyotism also requires attention to management literature's production of geopolitical anxieties, particularly in the shadow of concerns over the position of the "West" in relation to a rising "Asia." Too often accounts of Toyotism's management practices are severed from the geopolitical anxieties to which they contributed, in particular U.S. concerns over the rise of Japan and its increasing dominance over U.S. automobile production in the 1970s and 1980s.[2] Not so here. Managerial literature is a site in which anxieties about changing workplace models meet changing geopolitical winds. It is a site where geographical shifts in sites and modes of production meet micropolitical anxieties about workplace organization. Put plainly, these books make the global personal, for many workers, and put the personal and workplace micropolitics into dialogue with global shifts. The "global" and these shifts are not simply independent macroscale transformations of capitalism or the economy. They are complexly produced and managed by these management books, often written for a popular audience. This chapter takes inspiration from the work of Arif Dirlik, Alan Liu, Nigel Thrift, and Melissa Gregg in attending to the cultural and organizational effects of management literature on people, on media, on the workplace, and on the very form of capitalism (Dirlik 1997; Liu 2004; Gregg 2018; Thrift 2005).

Toyotism is a crucial managerial revolution for its development of the just-in-time logic that is the practical and conceptual basis of the logistics revolution, the gig economy, and platform capitalism itself. It is also a moment that reveals the role of management texts in at once provoking geopolitical anxieties and serving as a justification for new labor regimes organized around contingent, on-demand workers (the subject of Andrijasevic and Chen's chapters in this book). Toyotism's models of manufacture are one of the origins of the platform story and an overlooked source of inspiration for platform theory (Steinberg forthcoming). This chapter hence also serves as a reminder that the platform story can't be told without accounting for the place of Asia, the importance of hardware manufacture, and the travels of management theory in the production of platform capitalism.

Toyotism's Mediations

Toyotism refers to a set of practices pioneered by Toyota in the 1950s and 1960s around the production of automobiles. Toyotism involves the following elements:

- just-in-time (JIT) production processes
- *kanban* cards and other feedback mechanisms throughout the production process
- worker initiatives to suggest adaptations to the production line
- continuous improvement to the production process (known as *kaizen*)
- rigorous forms of quality control
- tight informational loops between automobile dealers and salespeople and the factories and component producers themselves, making for a nimble, highly adaptive, data-reliant production process

This set of elements was known as the Toyota Production System (TPS) (Ohno 1988; Womack, Jones, and Roos 1990). These production techniques were subsequently adopted first by other Japanese automobile manufacturers, parts manufacturers, and other industrial sectors, and later expanded to North American, European, and Asian manufacturers of automobiles and other goods. Toyotism is one of the origins of the just-in-time manufacturing and distribution (via logistics) technique used around the globe. In this sense it is much more than a manufacturing technique, and has become the governing logic of production, circulation, and consumption as well, informing on-demand services like app-mediated food delivery (Chen and Sun 2020).

Toyota gained attention as it ate into the U.S. and European share of automobile sales from the 1970s onward. As writers flocked to the company to learn its secrets (some of which were merely adaptations of management techniques developed by the American W. Edwards Deming, who was underappreciated in the United States but revered in Japan), its innovations impacted production systems around the world. It was celebrated for its creation of a system of production that extends outside of the factory walls into its subsidiaries and supply chain, as well as into its consumers' households via regular salesperson visits (Womack et al. 1990, 66). Toyota positioned itself as an intermediary node in the flows of information from consumers to the central production site, and then to subcontractors from there.

Feedback and the control of information were the basis for the principal innovation of Toyota: just-in-time. Ohno Taiichi (1988, 15), one of the architects of the TPS, describes the system as based around "the absolute elimination of waste": "Just-in-time means that, in a flow process, the right parts needed in assembly reach the assembly line at the time they are needed and only in the amount needed. A company establishing this flow throughout can approach zero inventory." Monden Yasuhiro, the foremost academic analyst of TPS, defines JIT as producing "the necessary units in the necessary quantities at the necessary time" (Monden 1994, 5). In contrast to the Fordist model of "just-in-case production" (Sayer 1986), wherein cars and their parts were produced just in case consumers wanted to purchase them, just-in-time is organized around small inventories, flexible labor with weak union protections, and the ability to quickly ramp up production if demand increased. Producing may be replaced by "procuring" here since it is a system that generally relies on external manufacturers to deliver items on time. It is a decentralized "pull system" in contrast to the central-planning "push system" approach (Monden 1994, 5–6).[3]

The goal was to regulate production such that only the minimum necessary number of cars are produced, using parts that arrive just in time for their use on the production line. This eliminated the need for "wasteful" storage space of parts on the premises. The main tool used in the elimination of waste and the operationaliza-tion of just-in-time was the *kanban* system. The kanban concretely refers to a paper sheet encased in a translucent vinyl plastic cover that allowed workers to order additional parts as they run low (a "production-ordering kanban"), or signal to a later process that fewer of a certain product are needed (a "withdrawal kanban") (Monden 1994, 36) (Figure 2).

The result was a kind of worker-led control over the production system. For this reason and others, Toyotism was often celebrated in English-language press as empowering workers and facilitating bottom-up control. As the assembly line moves in one direction, the kanban cards move in the opposite direction, informing internal and external factory suppliers what parts are needed and when, building a real-time data set about flows of supplies (Figure 3). Flexibility and anticipation of work were required of the workers as they not only assemble parts but also gauge when they will require more parts, or when they already have too many.

Store			
Shelf No. **F26-18**	Item Back No. **A5-34**	Process	
Item No. **56790-321**		**Machining SB-8**	
Item Name **Crank Shaft**			
Car Type **SX50BC-150**			

[Figure 1.2]. Sample production-ordering kanban (Monden 1994, 16).

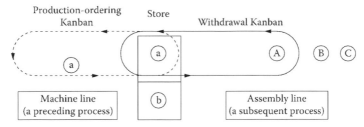

[Figure 1.3]. Illustration of kanban circulation process (Monden 1994, 10).

The circulation of information about production via kanban cards supported just-in-time production, which was in turn the core of TPS (Monden 1994, 9).

Ohno and Monden explicitly describe this as an informational or communication system. As Monden (1994, 15) puts it, "The *Kanban* system is an information system that harmoniously controls the production of the necessary products in the necessary quantities at the necessary time in every process of a factory and also among companies. This is known as *Just-in-time* (JIT) production." Or Ohno (1988, 51): "A kanban always accompanies the goods and thus is the essential communications tool for just-in-time production." It is also a means of surveillance inside the factory: "the Kanban system actually visualizes trouble in the form of line-stops or overtime," effectively surveilling the workers (Monden 1994, 27).

The kanban represents the medial and material form by which the management goal of minimal waste is achieved. Just as the punch card is a media mechanism for producing timely subjects and the means of calculating shift time, the kanban was the means of controlling the entire system of production such that there is never more inventory than needed. It was also a means of requiring workers to multitask: they had to both work on the assembly line and send inputs about inventory up the supply chain, anticipating the multiplication of labor forms under contemporary capitalism. Workers were also expected to assist in other tasks if workers at different points in the production process were slower than ex-

pected. Workers were thus information producers on the status of
the production line. The kanban card could be addressed either to
earlier processes inside the Toyota factory (Figure 3) or to outside
suppliers, in which case the card would also include a barcode and
delivery time for the item in question.

The simple physical object of the kanban card is also the material
mediator between the inside and the outside of the factory, the
means by which the main Toyota factory's many subsidiaries were
informed as to when their products would be due, how many, and
by what time. The kanban system enables Toyota to externalize
the responsibility to meet the production timeline to suppliers.
Given the massive size of contracts on offer and the penalties for
failing to deliver parts on time (as well as the complex financial
arrangements that sometimes gave Toyota part ownership in
the subcontractor via loans), the subsidiary was driven to deliver
on time, however difficult meeting such timelines could be. The
kanban system hence extended Toyota's control from inside the
factory over production timelines to outside control over subsidiaries, subcontractors and third-party suppliers, who were expected
to produce and deliver goods just-in-time.

Toyotism's cheerleaders celebrated the efficiency of its system. As
MIT management writers Womack, Jones, and Roos put it, Toyota
CEO "Ohno's idea was simply to convert a vast group of suppliers
and parts plants into one large machine" (1990, 61).[4] What they
ignore are the power dynamics built into this system and the
environmental consequences of the zero-inventory ideology. The
smooth functioning of the machine assumed kanban senders were
in relative positions of dominance in relation to kanban receivers,
which were often subcontracting companies. Subcontractors were
expected to produce the items needed on demand and to deliver
them *on time* as well. Higher-level subcontractors were expected
to deploy the JIT system within their own factories. This system of
just-in-time production also required a complex logistical system
of just-in-time delivery (Kaneko and Nojiri 2008). Here we see,
moreover, the close intertwining of the JIT manufacturing logic

with a dependence on the separate, but roughly simultaneous, development of business logistics that systematizes delivery or "inter-organization move-store activities" (Lai and Cheng 2009; Cowen 2014).[5] These deliveries produced their own form of waste as "frequent transport and delivery every day is necessary" (Monden 1994, 18). Tatsuo Naruse (1991, 47) notes that Japan's auto manufacturers may, "in an extreme case, require subcontractors to supply parts eight times a day." This results in "increasing distribution costs, traffic jams, and destruction of the environment"— prompting the Japanese government to step in and mandate fewer deliveries per day. The JIT managerial ethos of reducing waste results in the production of *more* waste, *more* traffic, and *more* pollution—but externalized outside of Toyota's factory. The kanban system was a means of decreasing inventory by externalizing waste and risk of overproduction; it was also a means of surveilling the entire production process. The parallels between this and the current situation of Amazon's drive for optimization combined with the pollution of its delivery operations are striking (Stewart 2020).[6]

The kanban card was the material means by which Toyota constructed the system of devolved responsibility that allowed it to outsource much of the production of associated goods that went into the car. The Toyota factories operate as central hubs around which some ten tiers of subsidiary companies and subcontractors are arrayed. Kenney and Florida (1993, 46) estimate that 70 percent of production was outsourced while only 30 percent was produced in house. The kanban card as managerial technique also had social consequences, encouraging the reliance on precarious employment within the subsidiaries that had to take on the risks of production made to order, and also bore the consequences in the case of a dip in demand for automobiles and their parts. The core companies ensure guaranteed employment to their workers, whereas the further removed subcontractors depend on expendable, precarious, lower-paid laborers who were mobilized contingently to meet the fluctuating demands. These part-time and temporary workers were often women, minorities in Japan, and, after the reform of working visitor laws in the 1990s, temporary foreign workers (Allison 2014; Yamada 2010), who "make up the periphery of the Japanese economy" (Kenney and Florida 1988, 129). As Anne Allison notes, the "family-corporate system" of post-war Japan relied on a system of permanent employment for men, and "low-paid, peripheral jobs" assumed by women (2013, 25). The reliance on a contingent workforce composed of women's labor and the labor of a temporary foreign worker is also a preview of the increasing reliance on piecework and microtasks under digital capitalism, wherein "digital labour is experienced as a modern version of on-demand piecework" (Gregg and Andrijasevic 2019, 3; Lukács 2020; Nakamura 2014).

To sum up, then: the kanban card is an organizational media form that mediates an information system of production and extends a network of surveillance and control over the factory and its outside. Information moves unidirectionally down the supply chain to its ever more precarious workers and plants; finished materials move up the supply chain at the speeds and temporality set by the central Toyota plant. Communication through the kanban card is also thereby a form of control, as Mercedes Bunz (2019) would argue in a different context. There is, moreover, a gendered and racialized dimension of kanban's communicational control, between senders and recipients of the kanban cards. Male full-time workers in auto plants at the core are the senders, while women and migrant workers who do the piecework are the recipients, down the line, and through the mediations of subcontracted firms that send out their work for hire.

The generalization of management and its dispersal through the factory—where every Toyota full-time employee becomes a manager of the supply chain—proves the lie of the representation of Toyotism as a worker's paradise of gratified employment. Looking at the structure of the kanban card alone we see a power relation enacted between center and periphery, between male and female workers, and between the upstream senders of the kanban directive and its downstream recipients. The kanban card is mediation as a form of devolved managerial control and surveillance of the production system.

Toyotism's Mediatization

The kanban system had another form of circulation: as emblem of Toyotism and the terror of American and European carmakers in the 1970s and 1980s, as they saw their market shares decline and their fortunes wane in the face of the global rise of the Japanese auto industry. Toyota stood in for the Japanese auto sector in toto, and also for a larger economic threat posed by Japanese manufacture to Euro-American automotive supremacy in the 1980s. This threat was due to management innovation resulting in efficiencies in production and a greater reliability of the product; a penchant for making smaller cars suited to a post–oil shock moment where consumers wanted smaller cars; and supported by a yen pegged to the dollar until 1971, a monetary policy that helped Japan become an export economy. Japan's increasing dominance in automobile manufacture had an impact not just because the industry was important but because it was *the* symbolic industry of the twentieth century. Automobile production was the very site for the formulation of models of capitalism itself, such as Fordism, post-Fordism, and Toyotism (Urry 2004). The auto industry was also the locus for some of the crucial managerial innovations of the twentieth century that have reconfigured companies around the globe.

Japan's auto industry stood in for new ideas about production techniques, larger arguments about changes in capitalism, and the Asian threat to U.S. economic and geopolitical dominance. The peak of the first wave of this fear was the 1980s, when Japanese hardware companies battled out the VHS–Beta wars. The same companies later acquired major Hollywood studios, with Sony buying Columbia Pictures and Matsushita buying MCA (which owned Universal), provoking anxieties about the cultural takeover of the United States and, as the October 9, 1989, *Newsweek* cover had it, of "Japan Invad[ing] Hollywood." A protracted financial and property bubble saw Japanese companies awash in cash, acquiring symbolic real estate in New York, and provoking further concern of a generalized Japanese takeover of America. This was the era of peak "Japan bashing" (Miyoshi 1991), when U.S. publications knocked Japanese economic power in often explicitly racist terms. This exploded into overt racialized violence in a way that both builds on longer histories of anti-Asian racism (such as the "Yellow Peril" discourse) and previews Trump-era and post-Trump China bashing as well (something we address in the Coda to this book).

Management literature is a key site for figuring the Japanese challenge. By "figuring" I mean that management literature was a place of narration and a space of expression where authors imagined, articulated, incited anxieties about, reckoned with, and proposed solutions to the Japanese challenge to the American industry. Known in the press and management literature variously as the Toyota Production System, just-in-time, lean manufacturing (or simply lean), and zero inventory, Toyotism is a management technique mediatized. It circulated widely in the popular press, books, and management literature.

Focusing on books alone, this decade of Japan anxiety was bookended by the publication of Ezra Vogel's *Japan as Number One: Lessons for America* (1979), which proposed that "we learn something from the competitor overtaking us" and novelist turned right-wing politician Ishihara Shintarō's *The Japan That Can Say No* (1991). Between these we find books such as William Ouchi's *Theory Z: How American Business Can Meet the Japanese Challenge* (1981), Anthony G. Athos and Richard Tanner Pascale's *The Art of Japanese Management: Applications for American Executives* (1982), and Karel van Wolferen's *The Enigma of Japanese Power* (1989), among others, which either narrated the decline of the American industrial sector or followed Vogel in treating the Japanese miracle as something to behold. Most books mixed Orientalist and techno-Orientalist framings of Japan and the Japanese as a monolithic and culturally homogeneous Other. Japanese writers played no small part in abetting this stereotyping, offering their own self-Orientalizing discourses that mirrored these claims of Japanese homogeneity via celebrations of Japanese uniqueness (known as *nihonjinron*). The obverse side of American managerial fears of a Japan rising was a resurgent Japanese nationalism that animated many Japanese texts (Befu 1993), with Ishihara's *The Japan That Can Say No* foremost among them. Japanese nationalism is another side to the universal–particular dualism mapped onto the U.S.–Japan relation, wherein Japan depends on the United States (or the "West") for the construction of its own national identity. Naoki Sakai terms this codependency the "schema of co-figuration" (Sakai 2006), meaning—to apply his concept to the case at hand—that the figuring of the Japanese challenge in American management literature is always a cofiguration, a coproduction of Japan and the United States via this very body of writing.

Christopher L. Connery finds in the anglophone books of this period "an anxiety over knowledge . . . as the new commodity" (1994, 44). In fact, though, this anxiety was as much provoked by manufacture as it was by knowledge. In this sense, peak Japan anxiety found expression in a subgenre of the above books: popular and managerial works that focused on the automobile sector, and Toyota's innovations in particular. These aimed to operationalize the Japanese miracle for European and American readers. Books in this subgenre include David Halberstam's *The Reckoning* (1986), on the decline of the American automobile industry and the rise of Japan's auto industry; Richard Schonberger's *Japanese Manufacturing Techniques: Nine Hidden Lessons in Simplicity* (1982); and Robert Hall's *Zero Inventories* (1983), which narrated the lessons Japanese manufacturing could offer. These put the auto industry and Toyota in particular front and center in narratives of American decline and Japanese innovation. More academic studies like Alan Altshuler's MIT-based *The Future of the Automobile: The Report of MIT's International Automobile* (Altshuler, Anderson, and Womack 1984) followed. These books were joined by a series of books from within Toyota itself, or by its affiliated Japanese researchers, often in a rough English translation followed by a more polished version. These include Shingo Shigeo's *A Study of the Toyota Production*

System from an Industrial Engineering Viewpoint (1981; repub. 1989); Ohno Taichi's *Toyota Production System: Beyond Large-Scale Production* (1988), and Monden Yasuhiro's *Toyota Production System: Integrated Approach to Just-in-time* (1983; 1993).

The most popular and influential book on Toyotism was without doubt James Womack, Daniel Jones, and Daniel Roos's *The Machine That Changed the World* (1990) (hereafter *The Machine*). Based on research from the by-then decade-long MIT International Motor Vehicle Program but written for a popular audience, *The Machine* is the most frequently referenced articulation of Toyotism.[7] Funded by a North American and European automobile research consortium with a mandate to explain the Toyota system, it was written with an eye to showing not only the superiority of lean as a production system but also to showing "how any organization embracing the complete system of lean production can also win" (Womack et al. 1990, viii). In their unambiguous words: "Our conclusion is simple: Lean production is a superior way for humans to make things . . . It follows that the whole world should adopt lean production, and as quickly as possible" (Womack et al. 1990, 231). The book not only proves the superiority (in their account) of TPS to North American and European models of auto production still stuck in the legacy of Fordism; it also offers a roadmap for how to implement TPS outside of Japan.

This promise of implementation is no doubt a crucial reason for its success. The widespread uptake of this book has itself been the subject of several scholarly articles devoted to unpacking the reasons why, despite earlier works on the subject, it is *The Machine* that is most frequently credited with "disseminating the [just-in-time] concept outside of Japan" (Holweg 2007, 420). One of the book's other significant achievements is its popularization of the concept of "lean." Coined in 1988 but popularized by *The Machine,* "lean" became the keyword most associated with Toyotism in the Anglophone context. Alongside kanban and JIT, lean assumed a life of its own, moving from manufacture and supply-chain research in the late 1980s to early '90s, to aerospace and electronics industries in the mid-1990s (Samuel, Found, and Williams 2015). From the 2000s onward, lean was expanded to sectors such as health, finance, defense, media, education, and software development. It even became a model for tech start-ups, which I return to below.

Many of these books on the auto industry are carefully researched, convincingly narrated tomes that frame industrial transformations in alternatively large-scale geopolitical shifts, or minute-scale industrial innovations. They are designed to either provoke concern in readers outside of Japan or suggest the boundless innovations of the Toyota machine ready to be copied. They are also part of a larger management-theory industry (Micklethwait and Wooldridge 1996), in which the books are both provocations and answers to geopolitical anxieties. Management literature installs a low-grade fear these very books promise to dispel.

To better understand how this dialectic of anxiety production and dissipation works, we may turn to Melissa Gregg's analysis of productivity literature in *Counterproductive.* Gregg suggests we should read these books and techniques as part of a general project of "immunization" in the face of cold capitalist climates. Peter Sloterdijk, on whom Gregg draws, frames practices of the self and indeed house building as practices of immunization—a form of protection from a hostile environment (Sloterdijk 2011). Gregg suggests we view "productivity practices as so many variations of this need for personal insulation. Productivity genres summon a membrane of protection against the aggressive climate of a capitalist economy and the private worries of an interior world" (2018, 18). These practices of productivity and the popular management books that communicate them are modes of coping with a changing, challenging world of corporate competition and personal instability. No wonder, then, that the "initial wave of mass-market productivity titles bears close relation to the first flush of corporate downsizing in North America in the 1970s" (Gregg 2018, 55). It was also at this moment that the "competitive edge of Japanese management techniques was a notable source of concern" (Gregg 2018, 56). The time-management texts Gregg analyzes function at this point as "a form of subjective training" (2018, 73)—a response to an uncertain (employment) future.

If the self-help productivity tomes that Gregg analyzes create a bulwark against the unknown, the work around Toyotism and the "Japanese challenge" that I've drawn attention to above are part of the wave of publications that are the source of uncertainty and anxiety to which these books respond. These works are complex in that they provoke concern about a changing world and the place of American industry within it, at the same time as they offer analysis of the Japanese production techniques that promise the reader a leg up on this same world. As Connery puts it: "Anxiety and stress have a newly dominant role in the daily experience of post-1974 economic life. Pacific Rim Discourse produces and offers a solution for that anxiety" (Connery 1994, 46). In both producing this stress and offering solutions, these works are part of the cold winds of existential "shellessness" that Sloterdijk (2011, 25) posits as a condition of modernity, this time more specific to America post-1970s. But they are *as well* the manuals for how to better build a managerial house to ward off the ill effects of this shelless condition. Lean manufacture, JIT, the kanban system: they are the prefab structures of house building in the Pacific century to come. They promise to be American managers' more lasting post-Fordist homes.

This condition is, therefore, geopolitically situated. Shellessness in the 1970s and '80s is a condition produced by competition between companies translated into a competition between nations. The specter of Japanese managerial techniques allowing Toyota to overtake General Motors and Ford and, by proxy, for Japan to overtake America is the text and subtext of these books. We might take this language of immunization—which requires a person to take a small dose of a given disease to protect that person from it—one step further, then. American managers required their workers to take a dose of Japanese labor management practices to immunize the United States against the Japanese challenge. Japanese management was the disease and the cure—a process I'll turn to in greater detail in the following section. These books are like the "time management self-help" literature Gregg analyses, insofar as the management practices described therein contribute to the sense of instability of existence that they seek to mitigate. They promise to unveil the advantages of the Japanese system, and thereby allow their anglophone readers to gain access to the secrets of Japan's success story. Alongside the winds of shellessness they announce are coming, these books also teach their readers new ways to build comfortable enclosures that protect against the coming storm, to immunize themselves from the industrial threat posed by Japan.

The *kanban,* TQC (total quality control), *kaizen* (continuous improvement), just-in-time, zero inventory, lean—these foreign words, abbreviations, and neologisms function like magical incantations that ward off the threat of a rising Japan and promise an increase in productivity for the manager's firm. These terms and the books that hawk them are where management's mediation meets the mediatization of management in 1980s North America.

Toyotism's Mobilization

The third aspect of managerial mediations occurs when the representation of management practices discussed above works back into production; when ideas of JIT or the kanban system inform new management decisions, or when management practices as mediated are transposed into new industrial milieus, economic sectors, or geographies. We witness this third aspect or moment in the mobilization of Toyotism to alter conditions on the ground for American workers. We could equally discern it in the mobilization of TPS in other sectors in Japan, and, as the next chapters show, variations on the JIT concept were deployed in Foxconn factories in Central and Eastern Europe and in delivery platforms in China. I stick to the American case here.

The previous section tracked Toyotism as a symptom of general anxieties about the status of American manufacturing in the face of Japanese industry. Yet there was another side to Toyotism: as a tool for American factory owners and managers to erode the power of unions and wrest concessions on work conditions and job descriptions from their workers. Fear of the Japanese threat produced anxiety from American managers, but immunization required far greater sacrifice on the part of American factory workers, who were expected to give up hard-won rights and labor protections to secure "America" from the external threat. In this third respect management theory was mobilized, cynically and instrumentally, to argue for lower wages and lesser protections for American workers.

Recall that one of Womack and his cowriters' main mandates in researching and writing *The Machine That Changed the World* was to understand Toyotism in order to facilitate its implementation in North American and European factories. Given that their interests were directly aligned with those of upper-level management, it is not surprising that they showed scant attention to what workers thought of TPS. They celebrate Toyotism as a boon to workers' autonomy and happiness, and yet they do so, as one critic notes, without a single quote from a worker in their entire volume (Mehri 2006).

Earlier analyses had framed Toyotism as a result of the unique conditions of Japanese culture, as a product of some unique Japanese characteristics such as obedience to authority or feudalism, or as a unique production system that could not be replicated elsewhere (as summarized by Dohse, Jürgens, and Nialsch 1985, 122). Given their research mandate was to make this system fit North American or European auto manufacturers, Womack and his collaborators had it in their interests to narrate TPS as something as mobile and geographically transposable as the kanban cards they described. Their message was one that would also have resonated with the wider calls within corporate America for downsizing and the casualization of the workforce that had intensified during this period (Hyman 2018).

The TPS arose under conditions that were both specific to Japan and yet also replicable elsewhere. It was made possible first and foremost because of a postwar truce between unions and management in Japan, established after a state-led suppression of union radicalism in the immediate postwar period and the ensuing "labor-management settlement" (Gordon 2017; Tsutsui 2001). Worker compliance was further enhanced by a familial corporate-management structure that required male workers to identify their interests with the company's. TPS required workers to manage stock, frequently change jobs, multitask, and adapt quickly to changes in the assembly line or the assembly process (Dohse, Jürgens, and Nialsch 1985, 120). TPS was a means of intensifying the control over workers; as Dohse, Jürgens, and Nialsch (1985, 128) put it, Toyotism is Fordism minus the trade unions and worker resistance. Job and skill types that were kept separate in American factories and elsewhere due to hard-won victories for the labor movement were, in the Japanese context, collapsed by design.

In managerial literature Toyotism was presented as a worker's paradise of bottom-up, continuous learning that made for happier, more satisfied workers. Workers were said to be their own bosses and active agents in the betterment of TPS. The reality was quite different from the myth (Masami 1994). Even apologists for Toyotism like Kenney and Florida acknowledge that "new penetrating forms of corporate control and hegemony appear to be required for the model's success" (1993, 306). Toyota's factories weren't workers' paradises but rather spaces of total social mobilization wherein workers were expected to express fealty to the company first and foremost.

Naruse (1991, 34) rather pointedly sees the framing of Toyotism as flexible and "suited to human nature" as based on "a lack of understanding about the conditions of workers and subcontractors" and an "underestimation of the suffering" that underpins the Japanese production system. Mehri, who worked in Toyota plant for a number of years, notes that the upbeat account of Toyotism offered by Womack et al. is not just wrong but dangerous. To Mehri *The Machine* presents a "gross misrepresentation of the Japanese work system" and is "a threat to trade unions everywhere" (2006, 25).

For these very same reasons, to American managers TPS presented not only an anxiety-inducing challenge but also an opportunity. An opportunity to convince workers that the rights they had fought for would have to be given up. If America was to compete with Japan, workers would have to multitask like the Japanese; send along kanban cards to monitor inventory, and identify with the company as if it was their family. Whatever threat Toyotism posed to American management, it posed tenfold to its workers. Toyotism and its supposed threat was transmuted into an opportunity for American car makers to undermine the unions whose strength had been part of the postwar capital–labor settlement, to demand workers take on more tasks and more work. If Toyotism presented a "threat to trade unions everywhere" (Mehri 2006, 25), this was also precisely what the managerial class appreciated about it. This is, then, the flip side of American managers' anxiety over Toyotism: ideas about TPS were mobilized in order to win concessions from workers and their unions. The organizational media of Toyotism—kanban and just-in-time—were ideal antidotes against the organizational efforts of another kind: American labor unions.

The opening of the NUMMI plant in California, a joint collaboration between Toyota and General Motors launched in 1984, was a critical moment in the mobilization of anxieties over Toyota to erode worker protections, and a frequent referent in *The Machine* as proof of Toyotism's transposability to the U.S. context. This NUMMI plant was GM's attempt to learn from Toyota, implementing the TPS with "no compromises on lean production" (Womack et al. 1990, 82). As Womack et al. enthusiastically note, TPS's foray into the North American market was premised on the dissolution of worker rights: "in place of the usual union contract with thousands of pages of fine print defining narrow job categories and other job-control issues, the NUMMI contract provided for only two categories of workers-assemblers and technicians" (1990, 83). The devastating impact on workers' rights and health in the United States is well documented by Mike Parker and Jane Slaughter who dub TPS "management by stress" (Parker and Slaughter 1988; 1990). In his account of three decades of lean, Christopher Huxley lists the following as "core problems" of the production model's implementations in North America: "work intensification, health and safety concerns, lack of seniority, lost job ownership, the disappearance of job ladders, and the absence of genuine skill development" (Huxley 2015, 149). As the NUMMI plant went from an experiment to being seen as "*the* success story in US automobile manufacturing" (Parker and Slaughter 1990, 31), it also was taken as a model to implement. NUMMI became a beachhead for weakening worker's rights in the North American context. In 2010 this very same NUMMI Fremont plant was acquired by Tesla and was renamed the Tesla Factory. Accounts of labor practices at the Tesla Factory (Wong 2017; Duhigg 2018) indicate that it operates (deliberately or not) through an intensified version of Toyota's "management-by-stress," making the factory one of the legacies of the TPS in the United States to this day. Later JIT became the modus operandi for the exploitation of workers around the world, as Rutvica Andrijasevic recounts in her chapter here and elsewhere (Andrijasevic and Sacchetto 2017) in relation to electronics manufacturer Foxconn's operations.

In this third moment described above, just-in-time and the kanban system are operationalized as generalizable logics of production that demand (conveniently for the managerial class) the weakening of worker rights. National anxiety about the rise of Japan becomes an excuse for weakening American unions; national cofiguration (Japan versus America) serves as a means of waging class warfare, with the managers undermining workers' rights. TPS is mobilized to justify worsening the labor conditions of the workforce and the management-by-stress in automobile manufacture and beyond. The kanban system and JIT are a source of anxiety for American managers at one moment, but at another moment they are mobilized to erode the rights and working conditions of laborers in North America. Ultimately it is the workers who bear the brunt of the reorganization required of this immunization project.

From Software to Venture Capital:
Toyotism's Afterlives

Toyotism started as a manufacturing technique and information-processing system that modulated production according to demand. Factory workers' tasks on the floor were mediated by the paper and later electronic kanban card, the centerpiece of the Toyota Production System. In its transpacific crossing, TPS was dubbed lean manufacture, a rebranding partly responsible for Toyotism's unlikely afterlives. In what follows I conclude this chapter by a telescopic consideration of two such afterlives: Agile software development and the lean start-up movement in Silicon Valley and beyond.[8]

Developing over the course of the 1990s, the main principles of Agile software development were formalized in an influential 2001 *Manifesto for Agile Software Development*. While this initial manifesto makes no direct mention of TPS, subsequent manuals of Agile software development do. The legacy of the TPS is present in a textbook by one of the signatories of the Agile manifesto, Jim Highsmith, which has a chapter on lean that directly quotes *The Machine That Changed the World* (Highsmith 2000, 289). Highsmith also cites Robert Charette as the original proponent of lean software development, having proposed the term in 1993, again based on *The Machine*. The Agile movement subsequently made lean software development a central principle, with most books on Agile adopting lean as one of its methodologies. One of the most prominent of these is Mary Poppendieck and Tom Poppendieck's 2003 *Lean Software Development: An Agile Toolkit.* Kanban itself subsequently became the object of several books on software development in the lean or Agile traditions (Anderson 2010).

Lean's next transposition was from software development to start-up philosophy. This comes via Eric Ries's bestselling 2011 book, *The Lean Startup.* As Francis Jervis explains in his analysis of *The Lean Startup,* Ries "credits Poppendieck and Poppendieck's *Lean Software*

Development (2003) as a bridge between the application of Lean principles in industrial management and the software industry" (Jervis 2020, 200). Ries's "hugely influential book" (Jervis 2020, 199) in turn had an impact on the conception of the start-up within Silicon Valley.

Fully accounting for the bleed of manufacture into software and subsequently into start-up culture is beyond the scope of this chapter. But the very brief account above draws attention to the ways in which software practices, start-up cultures, and platform business models in the present have hardware and even auto-motive legacies.[9] Toyotism is one locus of this set of practices that now lives on in start-ups from Silicon Valley to Shenzhen (Lüthje et al. 2013). It is also part of a set of reconceptualizations of knowledge work more generally. Alan Liu (2004, 46) notes the following aspects of knowledge work as articulated by business books in the 1990s: "ever quicker just-in-time production, riskier evaluation and pay schemes pegged to team- and company-wide performance, and, in general, what has been called management by stress." Whereas in this chapter I have focused on the kanban, Liu focuses on the team first and foremost, as a legacy of the impact of Toyotism on manufacture and on white-collar knowledge work. (The Microsoft Teams software is just the latest incarnation of TPS's team model.) Just as the team concept "deleted the entire apparatus of [job] classification earned through class struggle" (Liu 2004, 61) in automobile factories, this "deinstallation" of worker distinctions in blue-collar work is "transposed to managerial and professional levels" (Liu 2004, 62). Manufacturing work practices are made to fit postindustrial work environments. Toyotism is hence a key precursor to knowledge work and platform capitalism, as I argue in more depth elsewhere (Steinberg forthcoming).

Thus we come full circle from analyzing the kanban as a mediation for Toyota's managerial practice, to the mediatization of these practices amidst the Japan bashing of the 1980s in management books on or around Toyotism, to the cynical mobilization of elements of the Toyotist system as a means of eroding workers' rights. The last stage in this process, and a further media mobilization is in the entry of Toyotist lean manufacture principles into software development and Silicon Valley start-up culture via Agile, the Kanban method, and books like *The Lean Startup*. In this last stage, manufacturing principles are brought into the heart of the digital economy via software development and start-ups. Fittingly, *The Lean Startup* now circulates in translation as "a must-read book for all entrepreneurs"[10] in East Asia, encouraging readers to, as its Japanese subtitle has it, "Create innovation through a start-up process with no waste," or, in its Chinese subtitle "How to create a lean, sustainable, and profitable company." This transpacific circulation of mediatized management returns Toyotism's principles to its geographical starting point even as it has been transposed and transformed during its journeys.

To conclude, this chapter has demonstrated, via a close account of the travels of Toyotism as managerial model, that media studies must account for the models of mediation at work in the automobile factory, and the organizational effects and geopolitical anxieties that Toyotist how-to manuals and managerial texts produce across time and place. In following these multiple mediations of managerial practices we also see how the circulation of knowledge about these practices justifies precarious models of employment. Manufacturing methods from Toyotism reliant on technological devices, like the kanban card, inform not only the factory production of computer and smartphone hardware but also the software development methods and start-up practices equally implicated in the contemporary platform economy. As such the latent media effects of managerial mediations appear as manifest content in media platforms; Toyotism's implicit anticipations of the platform economy via just-in-time and the total surveillance of labor return via software manuals and start-up guides as its explicit blueprint— to say nothing of the parallel logics of "on-demand" video found in platforms like Netflix. Platforms as a managerial technology operating on a just-in-time, on-demand logic with an attendant precaritization of labor develops in no small part out of Toyotism and the global travels of its managerial model.

Notes

1   This approach differs from attention to the management practices *of* media industries, a focus of critical media industry studies (Caldwell 2008; Deuze 2011; Lotz 2014).

2   One exception to this is critical work around the concept of the Pacific Rim, taken up by area studies scholars such as Arif Dirlik in the 1990s.

3   Another concept Ohno highlights is autonomation, which Ohno defines as "automation with a human touch" (1988, 15). Note that I use Ohno's own preferred romanization of his name throughout (instead of the more standard Ōno).

4   Upon perfecting the use of kanban in automobile manufacture, Toyota used its sales network in a similar manner. In Japan it treated customer orders at dealers as the "first step in the kanban system, sending orders for presold cars to the factory for delivery to specific customers in two to three weeks" (Womack et al 1990, 66).

5   Lai and Cheng (2009) parse the distinct histories of just-in-time as a manufacturing logic from logistics as a discipline concerned with "move-store" activities, or distribution. Cowen argues that there is a common American military origin for both JIT and logistics (Cowen 2014, 30–31). While she is right that Toyotism is indebted to a series of time-management practices passed onto Japanese industry during the American Occupation, it is not a direct outcome of these practices, nor directly of military lineage. The model for JIT is rather a commercial one, inspired by the supermarket (Ohno 1998, 98) and not the military supply chain. JIT and logistics do go hand-in-glove, but they have distinct genealogies.

6   The example of Amazon or convenience stores like 7-Eleven (in Japan) makes visible the transposition of just-in-time from a logic of production to one of delivery for consumption (Steinberg 2019b). Dickinson (2016) addresses the supply chain logic as a crucial part of cultural production as well.

7   As one measure, *The Machine* counts 20,069 references on Google Scholar, versus 9119 for Ohno's *Toyota Production System.*

8   In directing my research for this section I would like to acknowledge the helpful suggestions of software developers Yvonne Lam and Stuart Marks. I also benefited from reading Francis Jervis's (2020) dissertation chapter on the lean start-up, which also maps the history of Agile software development.

9   This corroborates Ursula Huws's observation that platformed labor is in fact the instantiation of transformations much longer in timescale: "online platforms represent an extreme form of practices that have been becoming established in mainstream organizations across many sectors of the economy over decades" (Huws 2017, 41).

10 This is the title of the top user review of the book on Amazon Japan.

References

Allison, Anne. 2014. *Precarious Japan.* Durham, N.C.: Duke University Press.

Altshuler, Alan, Martin Anderson, and James P. Womack. 1984. *The Future of the Automobile: The Report of MIT's International Automobile Program.* Cambridge, Mass.:
MIT Press.

Anderson, David J. 2010. *Kanban: Successful Evolutionary Change for Your Technology
Business.* Sequim, Wash.: Blue Hole Press.

Andrijasevic, Rutvica, and Devi Sacchetto. 2017. "'Disappearing Workers': Foxconn in
Europe and the Changing Role of Temporary Work Agencies." *Work, Employment
and Society* 31, no. 1: 54–70.

Athos, Anthony G., and Richard Tanner Pascale. 1982. *The Art of Japanese Management.* New York: Penguin Books.

Befu, Harumi. 1993. "Nationalism and Nihonjinron." In *Cultural Nationalism in East
Asia: Representation and Identity,* 107–35.

Beyes, Timon, Lisa Conrad, and Reinhold Martin. 2019. *Organize.* Minneapolis: University of Minnesota Press and meson press.

Bunz, Mercedes. 2019. "The Force of Communication." In *Communication,* by Paula
Bialski, Finn Brunton, and Mercedes Bunz, 51–92. Minneapolis: University of
Minnesota Press and meson press.

Caldwell, John Thornton. 2008 *Production Culture: Industrial Reflexivity and Critical
Practice in Film and Television.* Durham, N.C.: Duke University Press.

Chen, Yujie, and Ping Sun. 2020. "Temporal Arbitrage, the Fragmented Rush, and
Opportunistic Behaviors: The Labor Politics of Time in the Platform Economy."
New Media & Society. https://doi.org/10.1177/1461444820913567

Connery, Christopher L. 1994. "Pacific Rim Discourse: The US Global Imaginary in the
Late Cold War Years." *boundary 2* 21:30–56.

Conrad, Lisa. 2019. "Organization Is the Message: Gray Media." In *Organize,* by Beyes,
Conrad, and Martin, 63–87.

Cowen, Deborah. 2014. *The Deadly Life of Logistics: Mapping Violence in Global Trade.*
Minneapolis: University of Minnesota Press.

Deuze, Mark. 2011. *Managing Media Work.* Thousand Oaks, Calif.: Sage.

Dickinson, Kay. 2016. *Arab Cinema Travels: Transnational Syria, Palestine, Dubai, and
Beyond.* London: Palgrave on behalf of the British Film Institute, 2016.

Dirlik, Arif. 1997. *The Postcolonial Aura: Third World Criticism in the Age of Global Capitalism.* Boulder, Colo.: Westview.

Dohse, Knuth, Ulrich Jürgens, and Thomas Nialsch. 1985. "From" Fordism" to "Toyotism"? The Social Organization of the Labor Process in the Japanese Automobile
Industry." *Politics & Society* 14, no. 2: 115–46.

Fuller, Matthew, and Andrew Goffey. 2012. *Evil Media.* Cambridge, Mass.: MIT Press.

Gordon, A. 2017. "New and Enduring Dual Structures of Employment in Japan: The

Rise of Non-Regular Labor, 1980s–2010s." *Social Science Japan Journal* 20, no. 1: 9–36.

Gregg, Melissa. 2018. *Counterproductive: A Brief History of Time Management.* Durham, N.C.: Duke University Press.

Gregg, Melissa, and Rutvica Andrijasevic. 2019. "Virtually Absent: The Gendered Histories and Economies of Digital Labour." *Feminist Review.* https://doi.org/10.1177 /0141778919878929.

Halberstam, David. 1986. *The Reckoning.* New York: William Morrow and Company.

Hall, Robert W. 1983. *Zero Inventories.* Homewood, Ill.: Dow Jones-Irwin, 1983.

Highsmith, Jim. 2000. *Adaptive Software Development: A Collaborative Approach to Managing Complex Systems.* Reading, Mass: Addison-Wesley.

Holweg, Matthias. 2007. "The Genealogy of Lean Production.'" *Journal of Operations Management* 25, no. 2: 420–37.

Huczynski, Andrzej. *Management Gurus.* New York: Routledge, 2012.

Huws, Ursula. 2017. "Where Did Online Platforms Come from? The Virtualization of Work Organization and the New Policy Challenges It Raises." In *Policy Implications of Virtual Work,* 29–48. Cham, Switzerland: Palgrave MacMillan.

Huxley, Christopher. 2015. "Three Decades of Lean Production: Practice, Ideology, and Resistance." *International Journal of Sociology* 45, no. 2: 133–51.

Hyman, Louis. 2018. *Temp: How American Work, American Business, and the American Dream Became Temporary.* New York: Viking.

Ishihara, Shintarō. 1991. *The Japan That Can Say No.* Trans. F Baldwin. New York: Simon & Schuster.

Jervis, Francis. 2020. "Eating the World Iterative Capital after Silicon Valley." PhD Diss., New York University.

Kaneko, Jun, and Wataru Nojiri. 2008. "The Logistics of Just-in-Time between Parts Suppliers and Car Assemblers in Japan." *Journal of Transport Geography* 16, no. 3: 155–73.

Kenney, Martin, and Richard Florida. 1988. "Beyond Mass Production: Production and the Labor Process in Japan." *Politics & Society* 16, no. 1: 121–58.

Kenney, Martin, and Richard L. Florida. 1993. *Beyond Mass Production.* Oxford: Oxford University Press.

Lai, Kee-hung, and T. C. Edwin Cheng. 2009. *Just-in-Time Logistics.* Farnham, U.K.: Gower Publishing, Ltd.

Liu, Alan. 2004. *The Laws of Cool: Knowledge Work and the Culture of Information.* Chicago: Chicago University Press.

Lüthje, Boy, Stefanie Hürtgen, Peter Pawlicki, and Martina Sproll. 2013. *From Silicon Valley to Shenzhen: Global Production and Work in the IT Industry.* Washington, D.C.: Rowman & Littlefield.

Lotz, Amanda. 2014. "Building Theories of Creative Industry Managers." In *Making Media Work: Cultures of Management in the Entertainment Industries,* ed. Derek Johnson, Derek Kompare, and Avi Santo, 25–38. New York: New York University Press.

Lukács, Gabriella. 2020. *Invisibility by Design: Women and Labor in Japan's Digital Economy.* Durham, N.C.: Duke University Press.

Manifesto for Agile Software Development. 2001. https://agilemanifesto.org.

Masami, Nomura. 1994. "The Myths of the Toyota System." *AMPO Japan-Asia Quarterly Review* 25 no. 1: 18–25.

Mehri, Darius. 2006. "The Darker Side of Lean: An Insider's Perspective on the Realities of the Toyota Production System." *Academy of Management Perspectives* 20, no. 2: 21–42.

Micklethwait, John, and Adrian Wooldridge. 1996. *The Witch Doctors: Making Sense of the Management Gurus.* New York: Times Books.

Miyoshi, Masao. 1991. *Off Center: Power and Culture Relations between Japan and the United States.* vol. 11. Cambridge, Mass.: Harvard University Press.

Monden, Yasuhiro. 1994. *Toyota Production System: An Integrated Approach to Just-In-Time.* London: Chapman & Hall.

Morris, Narrelle. 2013. *Japan-Bashing: Anti-Japanism since the 1980s.* New York: Routledge.

Nakamura, Lisa. 2014. "Indigenous cCircuits: Navajo Women and the Racialization of Early Electronic Manufacture." *American Quarterly* 66, no. 4: 919–41.

Naruse, Tatsuo. 1991. "Taylorism and Fordism in Japan." *International Journal of Political Economy* 21, no. 3: 32–48.

Ohno, Taiichi. 1988. *Toyota Production System: Beyond Large-Scale Production.* Portland, Ore.: Productivity Press.

Ouchi, William G. 1981. *Theory Z: How American Business Can Meet the Japanese Challenge.* Reading, Mass: Addison-Wesley.

Parker, Mike, and Jane Slaughter. 1988. "Management by Stress." *Technology Review* 91, no. 7: 37–44.

Parker, Mike, and Jane Slaughter. 1990. "Management-by-Stress: The Team Concept in the US Auto Industry." *Science as Culture* 1, no. 8: 27–58.

Poppendieck, Mary, and Tom Poppendieck. 2003. *Lean Software Development: An Agile Toolkit:* Reading, Mass: Addison-Wesley.

Ries, Eric. 2011. *The Lean Startup.* New York: Crown Business.

Sakai, Naoki. 2006. "Translation." *Theory, Culture & Society* 23, no. 2–3: 71–78.

Samuel, Donna, Pauline Found, and Sharon J. Williams. 2015. "How Did the Publication of the Book "The Machine That Changed the World" Change Management Thinking? Exploring 25 Years of Lean Literature." *International Journal of Operations & Production Management* 35, no. 10: 1386–407.

Sayer, Andrew. 1986. "New Developments in Manufacturing: The Just-in-Time System." *Capital & Class* 10, no. 3: 43–72.

Schonberger, Richard. 1982. *Japanese Manufacturing Techniques: Nine Hidden Lessons in Simplicity.* New York: Simon and Schuster.

Shingo, Shigeo. 1989. *A Study of the Toyota Production System: From an Industrial Engineering Viewpoint.* Trans. Andrew P Dillon. Portland: Routledge.

Sloterdijk, Peter. 2011. *Bubbles: Microspherology.* Trans. Wieland Hoban. Los Angeles, Calif., and Cambridge, Mass.: Semiotext(e); distributed by MIT Press.

Steinberg, Marc. 2019a. *The Platform Economy: How Japan Transformed the Consumer Internet.* Minneapolis: University of Minnesota Press.

Steinberg, Marc. 2019b "Delivering Media: The Convenience Store as Media Mix Hub."

30   In *Point of Sale: Analyzing Media Retail*, ed. D. Johnson and D. Herbert, 239–55. New Brunswick, N.J.: Rutgers University Press.

Steinberg, Marc. Forthcoming. "From Automobile Capitalism to Platform Capitalism: Toyotism as a Prehistory of Digital Platforms." *Organization Studies*.

Stewart, Jack. 2020. "If You Think Delivery Trucks Contribute to Road Congestion Now . . . Just Wait." *Marketplace,* January. https://www.marketplace.org/2020/01/15/if-you-think-delivery-trucks-contribute-to-road-congestion-now-just-wait/.

Thrift, Nigel. 2005. *Knowing Capitalism.* Thousand Oaks, Calif.: Sage.

Tomaney, John. 1994. "A New Paradigm of Work Organization and Technology?" In *Post-Fordism—A Reader,* ed. A. Amin, 157–94. Oxford: Blackwell.

Tsutsui, William M. 2001. *Manufacturing Ideology: Scientific Management in Twentieth-Century Japan.* Princeton, N.J.: Princeton University Press.

Urry, John. 2004. "The 'System' of Automobility." *Theory, Culture & Society* 21, no. 4–5: 25–39.

Van Wolferen, Karel. 1989. *The Enigma of Japanese Power: People and Politics in a Stateless Nation.* New York: Alfred A. Knopf.

Vogel, Ezra F. 1979. *Japan as Number One: Lessons for America.* Cambridge, Mass.: Harvard University Press.

Wasson, Haidee. 2021. *Everyday Movies: Portable Film Projectors and the Transformation of American Culture.* Oakland: University of California Press.

Womack, James P., Daniel T. Jones, and Daniel Roos. 1990. *The Machine That Changed the World.* New York: Simon and Schuster.

Wong, Julia Carrie. 2017. "Tesla Factory Workers Reveal Pain, Injury, and Stress: 'Everything Feels like the Future but Us.'" *The Guardian,* May 18.

Yamada, Masahiko. 2010. "The Current Issues on Foreign Workers in Japan." *Japan Labour Review* 7, no. 3: 5–18.

2

"Just-in-Time Labor": Time-Based Management in the Age of On-Demand Manufacturing

Rutvica Andrijasevic

Whoever can offer goods in the shortest time wins.
—Arthur Chen, ASUS Czechia

As I approached the reception at the workers' dormitory in Nitra, Slovakia, there were several large clocks in full view behind the reception counter. They showed the time in five different cities across Slovakia and Czechia: Prague, Bardejov, Brno, Nitra, and Pardubice (Figure 1). While to a casual observer these cities might not tell much, to those in the know the message is clear: they are the locations of some of the most important manufacturing sites for electronics and automobile assembly in Central and Eastern Europe (CEE). Nitra in Slovakia and Pardubice in Czechia are where Foxconn, the world's largest electronics assembler and the firm at the center of this chapter, located its European plants. The dormitory at the outskirts of Nitra is just about ten minutes' drive from Foxconn's assembly plant. It accommodates migrant workers assembling electronics hardware and is managed by Xawax, a temporary-work agency that supplies workers to Foxconn and other factories across Slovakia and Czechia. I use the clocks in this migrant workers' dormitory as the analytical point of departure to examine media forms through which time gets organized and the workforce managed in global electronics manufacturing.

Recently, time has emerged as a focus of scholarly analysis of digital economy and platform labor. Discussing the ways in which the platform economy operates, scholars have illustrated how a new temporal order, established though algorithmic control and enforced by customers' expectations of timely service delivery, is impelling workers to increase their labor productivity while, at the same time, worsening their working conditions (Chen and Ping 2020). With the attention placed on digital technology, firms that have so far been the center of scholarly analysis are either platform-mediated businesses such as Uber, Taskrabbit, and Amazon Mechanical Turk (Irani 2015; Prassl and Risak 2015; Sharma 2017b) or outsourced information technology–based businesses such as call centers providing software development and website maintenance (Aneesh 2009; Nadeem 2009). Studies of time management have made a pivotal contribution to our understanding of how digital technology generates new temporalities that configure people's perception of time and engender work arrangements that exclude the workforce from labor and social protection. Yet, current scholarly approaches to digital labor are problematic because they risk establishing artificial dichotomies between consumption and production, on the one hand, and digital labor and manufacturing, on the other. My argument is that this in turn overlooks the dependencies between software and hardware as well as the similarities in time-based management practices between digital and manufacturing labor. As Qiu (2017) and Steinberg (2019) convincingly show, both the digital media industry and today's digital platforms are anchored in manufacturing.

I deploy the term "just-in-time labor" (JITL) in order to illustrate the interdependency between media and management for time-based management of labor. Similar to the platform-mediated on-demand economy, electronics assembly is driven by an on-demand market imperative. The general trend in electronics manufacturing is time-based competition driven by a shortening of product life cycle and price erosion. This in turn has resulted in the adoption of so-called just-in-time (JIT) manufacturing, pioneered in the auto industry and typified by flexible and lean production (Pawlicki 2017). Time-based competition is organized, I suggest, via a diverse set of mediations such as labor intermediaries, dormitories, and social-media platforms (e.g., Viber and Facebook) that, while apparently not related, all join up in actualizing a very specific social order and relations of production. A close analysis of how time is mediated, either via institutional, discursive, or social processes, exposes the ways in which the JITL model engenders novel forms of work practices that further the vulnerability and exploitation of workers. While there has been some research on how the existing regulatory framework enables labor exploitation within supply chains (Andrijasevic and Novitz 2020; Howe and Owens 2016; LeBaron and Phillips 2018), a discussion of how the supply and assembly of labor is synchronized to JIT manufacturing is still missing. This synchronization, moreover, relies crucially on forms of digital mediation.

To examine how time-based management practices are enacted via different media, I draw on management studies, media studies, and feminist sociologists' theorizations of time. I establish these interdisciplinary connections for two main reasons. First, contrary to management scholars who examine gig work for its implications on standard employment relationships (Gandini 2019; Graham, Hjorth, and Lehdonvirta 2017), sociologists and media scholars showed that platforms operationalize a very specific idea of time, that of "real-time," embedded in the economic and utilitarian philosophy of time (Hope 2016; Wajcman and Dodd 2017). It is pivotal, I suggest, to understand this currently dominant philosophy of time in order to examine how it translates into historically specific practices of management. In doing so we see the impact of media transformations on labor management practices. Real-time is, after all, a temporality closely associated with the internet. Second, orthodox supply-chain scholarship commonly focuses on the synchronization of technical aspects of production so as to

34 achieve efficiencies (for an example, see Holl, Pardo, and Rama 2009). In so doing, it severs the tie between labor and technology and, as a consequence, disembodies time (Grappi 2020) and overlooks the violence of logistics on bodies (Cowen 2014). I draw on feminist theories in order to indicate how time is always lived and how it operates as a form of social difference (Sharma 2017b). For feminist scholars, globally organized systems of production not only perpetuate structural inequalities at the level of time but also rely, for their very existence, on the exploitation and performance of non-economic differences. As Anna Tsing has argued, "supply chain capitalism" (2009) mobilizes difference—gender, sexuality, citizenship status—to structure global production processes and extract value from labor.

To highlight the concrete nature of these experiences, I base my discussion on the original fieldwork my collaborators and I conducted of electronics assembly in CEE.[1] Our fieldwork took place

[Figure 2.1]. Photograph taken by the author at the workers' dormitory in Nitra, Slovakia. The clocks display the time in five different cities across Slovakia and Czechia: Prague, Bardejov, Brno, Nitra, and Pardubice.

in Czechia, Slovakia, Hungary, Turkey, and Serbia over the years 2012–2019 and focused primarily on the working conditions and labor recruitment practices in electronics assembly at Foxconn, and to a lesser degree at Samsung. While the bulk of interviews were with workers (70), we also interviewed managers and key informants on public institutions such as labor ministers, trade unions, labor inspectorates, labor offices, local job centers, vocational schools, and NGOs (40). We adopted ethnographic methods with a strong emphasis on participant observations, such as living in the dormitories and sharing workers' facilities, which are best suited to examine how time-based managerial practices govern labor and life.

Time-Mediated Competition

Time-based competition, operationalized via the JIT method, is a defining feature of electronics assembly. As Marc Steinberg discusses in chapter 1, JIT was pioneered in the auto industry, especially seen in what we know as Toyotism, and is typified by flexible and lean production. Contrary to Fordism, which is based on the principle of mass production and a "just-in-case" logic of overproduction (Sayer 1986, 43), Toyotism aims at maximizing profit by minimizing the production time. The JIT has also been named "zero inventories" because parts arrive to the production line only when they are needed. As Nishimoto Ikuko (2002, 104) put it concisely: "[JIT's] basic idea is to produce what is needed, at the time needed, and in the quantity needed." In order to save costs and achieve synchronization between material, labor, and machinery, JIT aims at eliminating "unproductive time" in assembly (Nishimoto 2002, 105) by reorganizing the sequence of work and speeding up production via computerized control. This in turn achieves a very high flexibility in the management of worker time and variation in the quantity in production. While the application of JIT is localized, taking place at the plant level, it allows for a dispersed yet tightly controlled production model due to the increased reliance on supply-chain and internal inventory-management systems (Steinberg 2019).

JIT systems are apt for electronics manufacturing in that electronics supply chains, while globally dispersed, are characterized by a modular governance structure that is managed across long distances through "codification" (Bair and Mahutga 2012, 277). This codified system enables labor-management practices to be scalable across geographies. Importantly for our discussion, such codification predates the common understanding of algorithmic control of labor typically attributed to the rise of digital platforms.

A key feature of the electronics industry is the vertical disintegration between product innovation and manufacturing. Lead firms—such as Apple, Hewlett-Packard, and Sony—focus on product development and marketing, while contract manufacturing companies—such as Foxconn—specialize in the assembly of hardware. Such a model is characterized by a significant imbalance of power and differences in profit between lead firms and their suppliers/contractors. Lead firms outsource higher-cost and higher-risk aspects of production and distribution to the contractors and decide on what goods get produced and where (Azmeh and Nadvi 2014). This creates intense commercial pressure on the conditions of price along the chain that, coupled with low profit margins available to the contractors, places downward pressure on wages and working conditions in assembly (Lüthje et al. 2013). Time is therefore crucial for contractors not only to meet client's demands but also to reappropriate some of the value captured by lead firms. Foxconn's operations in CEE illustrate this process well.

Taiwanese-owned, Foxconn's manufacturing headquarters are in mainland China, where it commands circa one million workers. In early 2000, Foxconn expanded its production from China to CEE in order to be in proximity to its Western European markets. It set up two factories in Czechia and one each in Slovakia, Hungary, and Turkey. There it assembles desktops, laptops, TVs, cartridges, and servers mostly for its main client Hewlett-Packard (HP) as well as for Sony, CISCO, Chimei, and Innolux. Electronics assembly plants in CEE are thus best viewed not as autonomous but rather as interconnected "nodes" (Coe et al. 2004) within the firm's

transnational networks of production (Figure 2). Being in proximity
to its customer markets in Western Europe has enabled Foxconn
to cut lead time required for products to be shipped from China
to Europe from twenty-two to two days. Jim Chang, Foxconn's
former managing director in Czechia, explained the firm's decision
to set up assembly plants in CEE as follows: "Time and distance
are crucial for business competitiveness. We need to be close to
our major market and deliver products within 48 hours of receipt
of a customer's order." As Chang further explains, "The products
we manufacture in the morning [in Czechia] can be halfway to
European Union customers by the evening" (CzechFocus 2007). In
other words, firms expand internationally in order to compress
space and time so as to be closer to their end-consumer markets
and be able to meet, in the shortest time possible, the production
needs of their clients.

Time-mediated competition is additionally driven by the fact that
electronics assembly is a highly cyclical market, characterized by
phases of high production volumes that alternate with phases of
average or very low demand. For example, periods of high demand
are quite regular and predictable, as these correspond to fixed
retail dates known well in advance such as Christmas, Black Friday
in the United States, 11/11 in China, back-to-school, new product

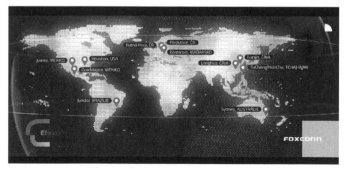

[Figure 2.2]. Foxconn's visualization of its interconnected manufacturing "nodes"
(source: Foxconn Czech Republic Linkedin post).

38   launch dates, and so on. These periods require contract manufacturers to have in place above-average manufacturing capabilities
for a limited—usually rather short—period of time. Consequently,
contract manufacturers put in place a flexible labor system that
enables them to respond quickly and to avail themselves of
sufficient workforce on short notice so as to fulfill last-moment
orders (Pawlicki 2017). Conversely, such a model needs to account
also for periods of low production and hence the ability to radically
decrease the numbers of workers once the orders from lead
firms fall.

Insights from management studies are helpful here to better
understand how firms minimize the costs of production and
respond to fluctuation of orders. Firms typically divide their
workforce into workers directly employed and those contracted
via temporary work agencies (TWAs). TWAs are used to manage
fluctuations in productive activity, externalize costs and regulatory
risks, and reduce contractual responsibilities of direct employment
(Theodore and Peck 2002; Thommes and Weiland 2010). As TWAs
are often unable to find workers in sufficient numbers locally, this
demand is met by a migrant workforce. The structural significance
of temporary workers for the electronics industry is best conveyed
by the fact that in January 2017, the Samsung plant in Slovakia had
570 permanent and 1000 agency workers.[2] As Barrientos (2013,
1066) put it succinctly, "The labour contracting system is [. . .]
integral to the flexible commercial functioning of GPNs [Global
Production Networks] across borders in a liberalised global economy." Temporary workers fulfill industries' need for an "on-demand"
workforce that can be "assembled" on short notice when orders are
high. Conversely, when orders are low, workers can be "let go" on
equally short notice. Workers are themselves treated according to
the logic of assembly familiar to us from JIT manufacture.

Hence, the temporary staffing industry provides firms with
flexible labor-management systems. Similar to platforms, which
are commonly defined as intermediaries, TWAs are mediators or
"matchmakers" (Evans and Schmalensee 2016) between firms and

workers. Accordingly, Niels van Doorn suggests that businesses
like Uber and Handy should not be seen as tech companies but
rather as platform labor intermediaries and as new players in
the dynamic temporary staffing industry (van Doorn 2017). They,
for example, fabricate a shortage of workers via "benching," the
practice of temporarily taking out of the labor market a specific
profile of workers in order to spur the demand (Xiang 2007),
or operate a comprehensive cross-border management of the
migrant workers (Andrijasevic and Sacchetto 2017). A key characteristic of these new players, whether they are TWAs or platforms,
is that they act as "market makers" (Coe, Jones, and Ward 2010),
and as such they reconstitute the labor market and labor relations.
How this is operationalized via several media forms that span from
platform-mediated recruitment, to management of information
about demands and whereabouts of job candidates, and finally to
dormitories as mediated environments is discussed later in this
chapter. I now first address the conception of time that underpins
global supply chains and JIT manufacture.

Real-Time

In a global production network, the management of objects (com-
modities), bodies (labor), and information cannot be separated.
Time-mediated management practices that aim at achieving the
synchronization of information, labor, machinery, and materials,
operationalize a very specific idea of time. This idea of time is best
known as "real-time." Real-time, as Wayne Hope (2006) suggested,
is a result of the interaction between globalizing capitalism and
digital technologies. The proliferation of information and communication technologies (ICTs) has engendered a new temporality
that has been referred to as real-time or "network time" (Nadeem
2009, 22). ICTs in conjunction with internet time has given rise to a
concept of real-time that permeates production as much as media
consumption. Mary Ann Doane, for instance, notes a shift in temporalities of consumption from television's emphasis on "liveness"
or immediacy to the "real time" of the internet (Doane 2016, 319).

Transformations in temporalities of production have arguably preceded these shifts in consumption but are determined by a similar set of media conditions.

Electronic data transmission from the Electronic Data Interchange (EDI) systems adopted in the 1970s in industry onward to the internet today cannot be measured according to the parameters of the linear, sequential clock time, as the speed of communication is no longer assessed by the time taken to cover geographical distance (Hope 2006, 276). Barbara Adam (2006) conveys this change best when identifying ICTs time as instantaneous, simultaneous, and globally networked rather than durational, sequential, and globally zoned. The ICTs and digital media, by permitting a vast increase in speed and volume of data and money, function as "conduits" (Purser 2002) or as mediums permitting an instantaneous mode of production, consumption, and finance. Digital technologies globally interlink production, consumption, communication, and finance, thus underpinning the management of complex and technologically innovative production chains (Hope 2009).

Electronic information systems have allowed transnational firms to "decentralise operations while centralizing control" (Hope 2006, 284) by linking suppliers to sellers, tallying production to inventories, and checking the quality and speed of production across globally dispersed assembly lines. Protocols, conceived by Galloway (2001) in terms of controlling mechanisms for decentralized networks, have long played the role of interface and link, suggesting that the managerial thinking behind current digital platforms existed long before the technology of digital platforms as we know it (Rochet and Tirole 2003; Thomas, Autio, and Gann 2014). Software systems encode managerial roles in that they diminish the need for physical control of processes and workers, as control is now embedded in the system itself via the code. As work design and work processes are programmed so that only certain options are available to the workers, Aneesh (2009) shows that the role of the software code is key to the temporal integration of work and for governing globally dispersed labor. Aneesh (2006) coined the term "the rule of the code" to convey this algorithmic system of governance that, as Julie Chen has extensively demonstrated in her work on delivery, apps use to manage the workforce and sequence the labor process (Chen 2018; 2020; Chen and Qiu 2019; Chen and Sun 2020).

Real-time is thus best understood as a "temporal regime" (Purser 2002, 157) that is underpinned by the belief that technology can be successfully employed to achieve time optimization. The notion of real-time as instantaneous, simultaneous, and globally networked posits time as entirely calculative, functional, and fungible. The assumption that time is exclusively objective instantiates, as Wajcman (2019a, 319) suggested, an "economic-utilitarian philosophy of time." Driven by this quantitative approach to time, businesses pursue technology-enabled "'intelligent' time management" (Wajcman 2019a, 317) in order to achieve increased efficiency and profit. In our societies where time is calculated in relation to money, reducing and/or eliminating time lags, as JIT manufacturing attempts to do, is seen as an indicator of progress (Hope 2006, 286).

Real-time is operationalized by management practices that attempt to reshape the labor process by compressing time and space, transposing internet time to the world of laboring bodies and assembly lines. Transnational labor contracting, in particular, makes use of "time arbitrage" in order to extend the work time across borders to achieve a twenty-four-hour business cycle, hence exploiting "time discrepancies between geographical labor markets to make a profit" (Nadeem 2009, 21). Twenty-four/seven society is characterized by what Winifred Poster (2007) has called "reversed temporalities of work." Round-the-clock office hours, as in the case of the U.S. companies that outsource a variety of functions to India (e.g., technical support, processing insurance claims, data entry), has meant that Indian workers in call centers need to work permanent night shifts or that software programmers stay late into the evening for conference calls with New York (Nadeem 2009).

In order for workers in the United States and India to work effectively in the same time zone, the 24/7 global economy has

brought about the collapse of the work–life boundary for the
Indian workforce. Within this temporal order, certain populations
are required to "recalibrate" (Sharma 2017b, 133) their lives so as
to fit with the temporal demands of capital's labor arrangements.
The inequalities that "real-time" engenders have become painfully
visible at Foxconn's plants in Czechia at the time of the COVID19
outbreak, where workers, without proper protective personal
equipment (PPE), were required to keep the assembly going while
managers, not constrained by factory shift work or shop floor,
deployed software to speed up or slow down the production from
the safety of their private homes.[3]

The notion of real-time obscures, therefore, as Wayne Hope
suggested (2006, 276), a scholarly "reflection [on the] interests and
classes who benefit from real-time formations." Hope argues that
digitalized networks that enable the expansion of tech corporations are not just communication networks but rather, by fusing
information with money, they are the very foundation of contemporary financial systems. Hence, real-time networks are not just
an outcome of technological development but are shaped by the
interests of the dominant groups such as ICT companies, financial
institutions, and transnational corporations. These networks are
exercised through the activities of CEOs, exchange dealers, and system engineers. To put it briefly, real-time establishes and mediates
a temporal order that bolsters vastly unequal power relations.

Despite the ideological tendencies of "real-time" to expunge the
subjective and embodied experiences of lived time from the
quantitative and rational real-time narrative, the realization of
real-time work regimes is in fact relational as it is dependent on
those who "recalibrate" to the time of others. Yet, time and time
again, the development of key management theories has been
represented as free from difference and subjugation, and void
of conflict and workers' struggles. Melissa Gregg's (2018, 40–49)
investigation of the famous Hawthorne experiments in the 1920s
and 1930s challenges the dominant rendering of management
theories of motivation. She shows how the famous Relay Room

study, commonly viewed as the cornerstone study of productivity in the manufacturing era, was accomplished on the bodies of economically precarious young immigrant female workers. Many of these young women of Polish, Norwegian, and Bohemian background excelled in productivity and efficiency targets not because they were more suited to withstand the repetitive menial job tasks, as Elton Mayo maintained in the original study, but rather because they were breadwinners for their first-generation immigrant families and eager to avoid unemployment at the time of the Great Depression.

Similarly, in his discussion of the origins of JIT manufacturing, Bill Taylor (Taylor 2006) suggested that scholarly accounts of JIT failed to examine the extent to which the subordination of women's labor was central to the development of Toyotism. Toyota's JIT production model relied on a division of labor between a male permanent labor force and a generally female (and, later, migrant worker) contract labor in lower level suppliers (Kenney and Florida 1988, 129; Yamada 2010). Contrary to men who were on full-time, stable contracts, firms deployed women—many of them once full-time employees returning to work following childbirth—as temporary workers and often for an additional so-called baby-shift from 6:00pm to 10:00pm in order to cope with the expansion and contraction of production. Women were also disadvantaged on the shop floor due to the definition of what constituted skills: their dexterity was seen as an innate feminine trait, while machine minding done by men was seen as a learned skill and hence compensated by higher wages (Taylor 2006).

To sum up: rooted within objective, quantitative, and rational narratives of time, and dependent on technological mediations themselves conditioned by managerial innovation and system design, real-time temporal order obscures management's reliance on the differently classed and racialized bodies as well as on the gendered spatial division of productive, unproductive, and reproductive time. By turning time into a disembodied, quantifiable commodity, the notion of real-time erases labor from both production process and consumption. In the next section I work against this erasure by placing workers' bodies and their lived time at the center of analysis in the attempt to show inequalities, exploitation, and subjugation perpetuated by management in order to fabricate and assemble just-in-time labor.

Just-in-Time Labor

In what follows I examine how the notion of real-time is operationalized in JIT manufacturing via different media forms. In placing labor at the center of my analysis, I focus not on production alone but I also examine processes outside production proper that make JIT manufacturing possible.

Mediating Future-Oriented Production

The name Foxconn alludes to the corporation's ability to produce electronic products at "fox-like" speed (Pun, Andrijasevic, and Sacchetto 2020). Foxconn's global network of assembly plants enables the firm to simplify and optimize production and continually balance inventories with demand. Foxconn operates JIT production based on specific customer orders so as to cut costs by reducing storage or warehouse time and mobilizing the workforce accordingly.

Control over time is achieved via an increase in speed that is constantly communicated via the digital, real-time technology. To increase efficiency, this mediation reduces unproductive time while also intensifying the labor process. At Foxconn plants, the often trivialized and repetitive assembly operations are regulated through a high-speed computerized line. As a worker put it: "The shop-floor control system is a live system." The relevant data is stored on the computers that control the line. In JIT production, operations are broken down into micromovements to eliminate unproductive time and allow for internal movement of the workforce (in case of bottlenecks, operators can move from one position on the assembly line to another). Thanks to the barcode system,

computers make it possible to record the pace of production step
by step and identify which workstation and which worker has
caused a fault. This is why, in production, Foxconn deploys young
men and women, aged between twenty and thirty-five, who are
able to learn tasks quickly and sustain the speed of production
and the variation of tasks for longer. Intensification of the labor
process on the other hand is mediated by a specific manufacturing
technique that emerged out of Toyotist manufacturing known as
"Kaizen." More generally described as "continuous improvement,"
with workers modifying and improving the production process, the
Kaizen system, as a Slovak worker explained, colonizes the entirety
of working time as it requires workers not only to keep up with the
flow but also to continually try to improve it:

> In Foxconn there is this system they call Kaizen, that
> means that you have to do better and better each day.
> Kaizen system is everywhere in the factory. We work just-
> in-time production and we have no storage. I would like to
> say that just-in-time production is good for the business
> but is not good for the workers because when there are
> no orders, people stay at home and they work only a few
> hours. (Miklos, male, Czech, directly employed worker)

As the above quote suggests, in consumption-driven production
where orders are cyclical, manufacturers perceive workers as unproductive labor. This view of the workforce, as Louis Hyman (2018)
stressed, is best understood in terms of the managerial paradigm
shift since the 1970s from considering a stable composition of
employees as a resource to seeing them as a cost or waste that
can and should be eliminated. This shift toward the perception of
workers as a cost or waste corresponds to the Toyotist logic toward
inventory and investment.

To assure the availability of workers when the demand surges,
Foxconn in Czechia deploys a time-based mediation device called
the "hour-bank" system. The system requires that workers do a
total of 930 hours over six months. The hour-bank system is used

to organize shifts, and it has both a regulatory function with regard to the workforce (workers are rotated on the basis of the number of hours they have worked) and a cost-reduction function, as all hours are paid at the same flat rate. When there are no orders and workers work only a few shifts, they end up "owing" hours to the firm. Because their hours are calculated over a period of six months, the hour-bank system ties workers to the employer for this period of time, during which they are unable to leave. This system also postpones the payment of any outstanding overtime to the end of the six months (Andrijasevic and Sacchetto 2016a). Interestingly, Jenkins and Blyton's (2017) research on Indian garment factories that supply large brands examines a similar practice. Their study illustrates how managers use time as the workplace currency to deliberately construct debt relations. When workers are unable to work because of deficiencies in supply-chain management or infrastructural problems, they still receive their wage. However, they then "owe" the hours paid but not yet worked to their employer. Over time, the workers' time debt becomes so large that, in addition to working their normal hours, they are unable to work back the hours they owe to the employer.

What we can observe here is the logic of credit and advance consumption applied to labor time. In both cases, time-debt functions as a reserve of time that managers manipulate in order to temporarily bond workers to the firm so as to extract maximum value through the labor process and meet the fluctuating market demand. Time debt then serves as a mechanism of control over labor, as well as a buffer to manage transnational networks of production. Importantly, the hour-bank system and the making of time-debt are also mediation devices that function as interfaces between present time and future time, thus reserving workers' availability in time. This is achieved by separating potential labor from paid labor (the old binary between productive versus repro-ductive labor) in the temporal dimension. The hour-bank system enables the company to colonize and commodify (i.e. advance) labor potentials, or rather, workers' availability to work in the near

future by only compensating the time in the *present* production.
I suggest a time perspective on consumption-driven production
makes visible employers' pursuit of a future-oriented tendency
whereby they not only offload the risks of fluctuating demand onto
their workers but also view the stable composition of labor as a
cost and/or waste.

Labor Intermediation and Work as Service

"Internal" flexibility as discussed above takes place alongside "external" flexibility enabled by labor contractors such as temporary-
work agencies (TWAs). TWAs act as mediators that intercede
between potential workers and hiring firms; they provide firms
with temporary-agency workers, usually migrant workers, for short-
term deployment. TWAs rely on platform-mediated recruitment via
social media and messaging apps to supply labor quickly and on
short notice. For example, on January 2, 2019, an agency in Serbia
used Facebook to advertise that it needed 185 workers to leave for
Slovakia in the next one or two days. For any additional information, the agency asked potential workers to use the messaging app
Viber. The workers who qualified by testing negative for Hepatitis
C/D and having no criminal record received an induction lasting
a few minutes, and were then bused to their destination some
500–600 km away and across several international borders,
and finally placed in dormitories to begin work the next day
(Andrijasevic and Novitz 2020). In addition to procuring workers,
agencies also relieved the firm of workers during periods of low
production:

> There is a group of workers that are going back home
> today [February 26]. So, half of the Bulgarian workers
> are going home now and will basically be waiting for the
> extension of production. They will be back on 23 March.
> (Vassil, male, Bulgarian, agency worker)

Labor mediation operated by TWAs intensifies control over agency
workers who experienced the "dual control system" (Gottfried

1992) as they are controlled simultaneously by the agency and the assembly firm. By positioning themselves between firms and workers, agencies' mediation role extends to include advertising, selection, and recruitment of workers in the country of departure; cross-border transportation, direct management of production (including control of workers inside the factory), and management of accommodation in the country of arrival; and finally the return of workers to their country of departure during periods of low production. Such functioning of TWAs represents a major departure from the previous model of organized labor migration flows in Europe, where under the guest-worker regime, states arranged the recruitment and transportation of migrant workers while leaving the control of the labor process to the firm. The change is best described in terms of a shift from a model of state-regulated labor migration and mediation to a model of private and comprehensive management of the workforce, aimed at maximizing the "short-term utilization of labour" (Andrijasevic and Sacchetto 2017, 68). As Xiang Biao and Johan Lindquist put it (2014, 122) today "more than ever labor migration is intensively mediated." In its function as an intermediary between hiring firms and laborers, the TWA should be thought of as a "media" form in its own right, adopting Weihong Bao's (2015) model of the medium as intermediary, as discussed in Introduction.

Recent data shows that in the European Union (EU), short-term deployment of labor is more frequent than the classic long-term free movement of workers (Mussche and Lens 2018). For some workers, it is the only form of engagement available to them. One telling instance is the example of a female Croatian worker residing in Serbia. In the past four years (October 2015 to June 2019), she has been recruited eight times by different TWAs in Serbia for temporary engagements in Slovakia and Czechia. During this period, she worked in electronics, white goods, and logistics for brands ranging from Shin Hueng Precision to Samsung and Honeywell, over periods varying from several weeks to several months. Each of these engagements were "informal," meaning that even though workers signed an employment contract, TWAs did not register their workers as employed in workers' countries of origin, thus not paying social security contributions and depriving workers of the possibility of claiming unemployment benefits. Within these subcontracting chains, workers were often unclear about whom to contact in case of irregularities, due to the dispersion of responsibility regarding who might be their employer. For example, Serbian workers working for Samsung in Slovakia were recruited by a Serbian agency, signed the contract with a Hungarian agency, and then were paid by a Slovak agency while effectively working for Samsung. We can thus observe that, as a mediation process, subcontracting chains are intended to obfuscate employment relations, dilute an employer's responsibilities, and (re)configure the terms and conditions of work.

The entrenched web of TWAs and the expansion of short-term deployment of workers is facilitated by EU legislative frameworks, in particular by the Posting of Workers Directive (PWD). The objective of PWD is to remove legal and administrative barriers to trade within the European Union. Under EU law, posted work refers to a worker sent by their employer to work temporarily in another EU member state. Consequently, workers are only temporarily "posted" from one state to another, with the intention that they will briefly perform certain services for the agreed service provider in the host state and then return to their home state. While they are referred to as workers in the wording of the legislation, posted workers are not, under the law, exercising their right to the freedom of movement as EU workers. For instance, posted workers are not given the legal right that entitles EU citizens to look for a job in another EU country, stay there even after the employment contract has finished, and enjoy equal treatment with nationals in access to employment, working conditions, and all other social and tax advantages. Instead, their mobility is better described as the free mobility of services (Novitz and Andrijasevic 2020). I discuss the conceptual relevance of the shift from workers to services in the final section of the chapter.

As we can observe, the classification of workers as services erases labor once again. In addition to the notion of the real-time expunging of labor from production and consumption, the classification of workers as services removes cross-border labor from protections that the law ordinarily bestows. Insofar as posting is considered a movement of services rather than workers, posted workers are notionally regarded as not gaining access to the labor market of the state to which they move. In other words, the combined mediation by EU law and TWAs "disembeds" posted workers from the host country's institutional employment framework and from collective channels of representation (Hayes and Novitz 2013). Put differently, the legal framework dematerializes labor, rendering it mobile, flexible, and capable of being deployed just-in-time. Here, then, we see a return of the real-time model of mediation that effectively removes workers from their regulatory regimes in order to make them more mobile and available. Extending this argument, we can say that the mandate to operate in real-time affects not only the temporal availability of workers—that they be available to move anytime—but also effects a notional transformation of the work they perform, turning workers themselves into a service.

Unsurprisingly, these limits to regulatory protection and collective representation result for posted workers in substantial labor violations, such as lack of employment security, payment below the host country's minimum wage, above-maximum working times, bogus deductions for social insurance, and nonpayment of holiday pay and overtime (Alberti and Danaj 2017; Berntsen and Lillie 2016; Novitz and Andrijasevic 2020). In sum then, the posting relationship strengthens competitive subcontracting, favoring firms while constraining the rights of workers. Importantly, while it is possible to view employment-based migration policies as a form of labor-management technology, the case of posted work appears to have blurred the line between employment-based migration policy and trade policy. Mediated by law, this blurring of boundaries is driving new migration flows while concurrently reorganizing the labor markets and enabling new means of labor control and exploitation.

Dormitories as Repositories for Just-in-Time Labor

Managerial practices are, as we have seen so far, mediated by real-time technologies and devices and aimed at compressing time to achieve speed and efficiency. The compression of time goes hand in hand with compression of space. The operationalization of JIT production hinges on the use of collective dormitories. Dormitories enable firms to synchronize migrant labor to the needs of the fluctuating demands of production, as I illustrated in the opening image of multiple clocks and times. Reordering of work and life spaces, as I will show in the case of collective workers dormitories, merges productive and reproductive spaces so as to reduce "unproductive time." As per gendered construction of real-time, unproductive time is comprised of reproductive, affective, and housework intervals. Namely, it is the wasteful time when "nothing" happens production-wise.

Dormitories are key spatial mediations for the management of time with respect to migrant labor; they are a form of "organizational media" and media as environment (Beyes, Conrad, and Martin 2019; Beyes, Holt, and Pias 2019). Local residents live in houses and flats in villages or cities close to the factories. Migrant workers, on the other hand, are housed in different dormitories based on their nationality and the TWA they work for. As early as 2001, Foxconn in Czechia tried to build its own dormitories but gave up because of local opposition. The solution was to pass the responsibility for the dormitories on to the TWAs, who rented individual hotels, army barracks, or former factory lodgings to house the workers. These dormitories are all located off-site and across town, within both the larger city centers and the suburban outskirts. Some TWAs decided to build their own dormitories, such as the Xawax dormitory I described in the opening section of this chapter.

The type of employment contract used by the agencies relied heavily on the dormitories. Workers were initially signed up for a period of three-hundred hours, which functioned as a probation period, and were then promised a one-year contract. During the probation period, TWAs would postpone the payment of workers' wages: rather than being paid their full wages, they were given an advance of 1000 CZK (€40) per week. The promise of a one-year contract serves as an incentive to complete the three-hundred hours, which in periods of low production could take two to three months:

> The agency told us we would work twelve hours a day, every day, and that all we need to do is some operation on the assembly line. They told us we'll work six times twelve-hour shifts in a week and have one day off. When we got here they told us we wouldn't do twelve-hour shifts but actually alternate one short with one long working week. And then, we went to work today and we were told that there is no work. The scheduling clearly said that we are to work today. I woke up in the morning at 4am, went to the factory and they sent me back. (Pepik, male, Slovak, agency worker)

It was not uncommon for workers to have to wait a week in the dormitory without work. Given fluctuating production requirements, the dormitories enabled the agencies and Foxconn to stand workers down for several days without risking a shortage of workers. In addition to the pressed production period and intervals, I suggest that waiting is another key temporal dimension in the JIT manufacturing regime.

In contrast, during periods of high production, dormitories allowed the agencies to extend the workday, as explained by a Polish worker:

> When I was in the dormitory the coordinator would come, knock on the door, enter and tell us, "Let's go, there is work." He would grab us and we would need to go even if we just finished our shift. He would also wake us up and make us go. (Karol, male, Polish, agency worker)

Dormitories therefore operate as both environmental and organizational media (see the Introduction), in that they construct the environment pivotal to Foxconn's flexible organization of production. With no children permitted, dormitories eliminate any disruption caused by schooling or parenting needs, turning all activity toward meeting the production needs of the firm. Dormitories allow the firm to facilitate just-in-time, high-speed production by compressing the workplace and living space, lengthening or shortening the working day, and extending management's control over labor outside the workplace. Such control is enhanced through the use of information asymmetry. Based on existing retail patterns, Foxconn knows well in advance when the peak production periods are to take place, but agency workers are kept in the dark about the existing production dynamics. Dormitories thus help construct a workforce marked by what Gregg (2011) has called "work's intimacy," namely the anxiety and anticipation of work produced by the blurring of the boundary between work and off-work time.

While the assembly line and dormitories are both incorporated into the JIT labor management regime, dormitories are also socializing environments that facilitate the dissemination of information and expansion of workers' ethnic networks. Many migrants at Foxconn previously worked in other EU countries and, by relying on the TWAs and dormitories, were able to gain access to information about working conditions and wages elsewhere, move and find work relatively easily. This labor mobility enacted by migrant workers is producing a workforce that is more aware of the European dimension of the labor market, of strategies for moving from one country to another, and of how to obtain work in different EU states. Work experience in different contexts allows migrants to accumulate and share knowledge about labor migration, develop cross-country job-search strategies, and compare wages and working conditions experienced in various locations. Given their short-term contracts, lack of career prospects, and unpredictability of work availability in the electronics industry, EU migrant workers display weak attachments to the job and the firm. Experiences

54 of labor migration, cross-country job comparisons, temporary attitudes to their workplace and weak attachments to the firm all enable workers to exit unfavorable working situations (Andrijasevic and Sacchetto 2016b).

Today's dormitories are best viewed, I suggest, as repositories for JIT labor and as the organizational media required for the mobilization and control of JIT labor. They are material environments by means of which labor is managed. The systemic use of dormitories has a long history in the United Kingdom, South Africa, Latin America, and Asia, where dormitories were used during industrialization (Smith 2003). Workers—typically young, male, low-skilled or manual rural laborers—would live "at work" during the working week and return to their homes for the weekend. What is different today, compared with previous historical processes of industrialization, is that dormitories accommodate both male and female workers and are geared not toward securing a workforce for long-term employment but rather toward enabling the just-in-time model for the utilization of labor.

In today's JIT manufacture, firms use dormitories to mediate the contraction and expansion of production. Dormitories thus operate as media that temporarily capture and attach transient and mobile workers to the firm. In the context where workers have very little prospect of redressing their grievances either through the law or trade unions, exit from the organization and going elsewhere is a way for migrant workers to assert their "temporal autonomy" (Nadeem 2009, 35). In doing so, migrant workers reject ad-hoc work scheduling, firms' commandeering of their off-work time, and relentless downward pressure on wages and working conditions. The struggle over working conditions is, I would suggest, increasingly a struggle over time.

Producing Real-Time Workers

Focusing on how time is organized by different media forms—from Facebook to factories, TWA contracts to time debt, bus timetables

to dormitories—makes visible the extent to which JIT manufacturing rests on the construction and mediated control of a particular
kind of labor force. The workforce service supply described in
this chapter is summoned to meet a particular mode of efficiency
driven by the conceptual framework and concrete practices of real-
time. Consumption and production need thus to be approached
together in order to theorize contemporary labor relations and
account for divisions characterized by gender, citizenship status,
and geographical disparity that sustain exploitation in electronics
supply chains. After all, workers whose working conditions I have
discussed above produce the technology that allows for the synchronization and production of real-time. Similarly, recruitment
via Facebook and Viber extensively used by labor contractors im-
poses onto workers the expectation of just-in-time organizational
temporality.

Examining consumption and production together is crucial in order
to challenge, once more, the analytical binary between the manufacturing sector and creative labor, too often treated as separate.
The former is the domain of labor process scholars and the latter
of ICTs and cultural studies research. These disciplinary divisions
are currently being reproduced within the scholarly work on the
digital economy. Scholars who examine the labor process in the
gig economy do so strictly in relation to platform workers (see, for
example, Gandini 2019). Yet, such a binary mode of analysis is inad-
equate as it fails to observe that it is "circuits of labour" (Qiu, Gregg,
and Crawford 2014), composed of assembly, distribution, and
consumption, that enable smartphones to operate. Marc Steinberg
(forthcoming) suggests the studies of the platform economy that
posit its novelty fail to observe that the intermediary model of the
platform, nowadays the very base of the digital economy and gig
work, is traceable to initiatives undertaken by Toyota in automobile manufacturing in 1960s and 1970s Japan. Moreover, it is our
addiction to smartphones and social media that engender highly
exploitative and life-threatening working conditions in assembly
factories (Qiu 2017).

Taking this line of thought further, and building on the media-management intersections identified in the above sections, I suggest that there are significant similarities between platform work and manufacturing that, when analyzed side by side, urge us to conceive of conceptual continuities rather than divisions between various forms of labor. These continuities are best observed in studies showing that "lean" production methods typical of Toyotism are applied to white-collar service work (Nadeem 2009, 24). They are also visible in the research that compares operational modalities between temporary staffing industry and digital labor platforms (van Doorn 2017). An additional similarity can be drawn from my previous discussion of posted work, where workers doing manufacturing labor in sectors such as assembly, construction, and agriculture are legally classified as "services." The legal classification of large segments of the industrial workforce as services shows the arbitrariness of the neat distinction between the industrial and service economies and the spread of the "workforce-as-a-service" model (Starner, in van Doorn 2015, 908). This deliberate (mis)classification complicates the current legal debate on the employment classification of gig workers on digital platforms.

The regulatory domain in which work is placed is key for understanding the striking similarities of posted work with work in the service economy, platform-mediated or not. Posted workers, like gig workers, have no direct employment relationship, experience dispersion of responsibility in terms of who might be ultimately responsible for their circumstances, and are located outside trade union representation. All of this significantly limits workers' ability to claim or enforce their employment and social rights. As a result of the "platformization of work" (Huws et al. 2019), large segments of what used to be industrial work have been placed within the regulatory domain of the service economy, consequently limiting workers' social and legal protections and rendering workers extremely vulnerable to exploitation.

Given that platformization of work is tied up in labor intermediation, additional attention ought to be paid, particularly by media

studies scholars, to how technological objects bring into being
transnational labor-supply structures. Stephanie Barrientos (2013)
and Jennifer Gordon (2017) refer to these as "labour chains" and
"human supply chains," respectively, in order to convey the lack of
freedom and the subordination of labor within the transnational
subcontracting process. My earlier discussion on time-debt showed
how managerial practices of real-time instantiated several forms
of unfreedom: workers were tied into a contract with a particular
employer, living under a menace of penalty and/or nonpayment of
wages, subject to illicit deductions from pay, risking homelessness
because of their accommodation was tied to their work, isolated
by geography and language, and distant from any meaningful legal
protection. In other words, workers got caught in unfree labor
relations they may have entered voluntarily but found difficult to
exit. A temporal frame of analysis of JIT manufacturing thus makes
visible the extent to which, as Sarah Sharma (2017a) puts it, "the
reorganization of labour and vulnerability are part of the message
of every medium." For media scholars, this suggests an urgent
need to move away from a national framework of analysis and to
examine how workforce service supply, whether for gig work or
hardware manufacturing, is embedded within a novel geography of
transnational labor arbitrage that pivots on unfree labor relations.

One final aspect of the fabrication of JIT labor that warrants further
discussion is the gendered construction of real-time. My earlier
analysis of dormitories showed that dormitories operationalize
the notion of real-time in ways that reflect real-time's normative
gendered underpinnings grounded in the traditional separation
of productive, unproductive, and reproductive time and space. A
focus on dormitories reminds us therefore of the extent to which
Toyota JIT manufacturing in the 1960s, electronics export–oriented
manufacturing in the 1970s and 1980s (Elson and Pearson 1981;
Lee 1995), and today's JIT electronics assembly are all rooted in a
gendered division of labor. However, a focus on the dormitories
also reveals how globally integrated circuits of production hinge
on the appropriation of "unproductive" time. By appropriation I

mean the ways in which dormitories extract additional value from workers' "private" lives (Pun 2007). This is achieved both through the extension of management's control into workers' time and space off-work as well as the regulation of family life.

Workers' integration into a real-time global economy thus brings about what Aneesh (2009, 364) has called "a temporal unhinging of family life." Such unhinging exposes the gendered bias embedded within real-time's temporal order. Real-time operations are modeled on the lives of very specific subjects. These are "brogrammers," better known as Silicon Valley software developers who are typically young, white, and male and who cherish the myth of heroic individualism. These are also subjects that are unencumbered by the responsibilities of care (Gregg 2018) and who perceive the concept of work–life balance or private time as antiquated (Wajcman 2019b). A gendered reading of real-time thus renders visible what Barbara Adam (2002) has identified as "detemporalization of time," a term she uses to indicate the fabrication of utilitarian and calculative time disassociated from affective labor, care work, and housework commonly performed by women. The widespread tendency in studies on platform workers to study temporalities apart from gender division of labor risks overlooking how temporal and spatial reconfigurations of labor, characteristic both of supply-chain and platform economy, are anchored once again in gendered power relations and naturalized notions of reproductive labor.

Notes

1   The research project has been led by Rutvica Andrijasevic (University of Bristol) in collaboration with Devi Sacchetto (University of Padua), Pun Ngai (University of Hong Hong), and five research assistants: Marek Čaněk, Hannah Schling, Nuran Gülenç, Tereza Virtova, Tibor Meszmann.

2   Spectator Staff, "Samsung Will Shut Down Its Slovak Plant." *The Slovak Spectator*, January 29, 2018. https://spectator.sme.sk/c/20748727/samsung-will-shut -down-its-slovak-plant.html.

3   https://dversia.net/5949/corona-tsenajivot/.

References

Adam, Barbara. 2002. "The Gendered Time Politics of Globalization: Of Shadowlands and Elusive Justice." *Feminist Review* 70:3–29.

Adam, Barbara. 2006. "Time." *Theory, Culture & Society* 23, no. 2–3: 119–26. https://doi .org/10.1177/0263276406063779.

Alberti, Gabriella, and Sonila Danaj. 2017. "Posting and Agency Work in British Construction and Hospitality: The Role of Regulation in Differentiating the Experiences of Migrants." *The International Journal of Human Resource Management* 28, no. 21: 3065–88. https://doi.org/10.1080/09585192.2017.1365746.

Andrijasevic, Rutvica, and Tonia Novitz. 2020. "Supply Chains and Unfree Labor: Regulatory Failure in the Case of Samsung Electronics in Slovakia." *Journal of Human Trafficking* 6, no. 2: 195–208.

Andrijasevic, Rutvica, and Devi Sacchetto. 2016a. "Foxconn beyond China: Capital Labour Relations as Co-determinants of Internationalization." In *China at Work: A Labour Process Perspective on the Transformation of Work and Employment in China,* ed. Mingwei Liu and Chris Smith, 337–60. Basingstoke, UK: Palgrave Macmillan.

Andrijasevic, Rutvica, and Devi Sacchetto. 2016b. "From Labour Migration to Labour Mobility? The Return of the Multinational Worker in Europe." *Transfer: European Review of Labour and Research* 22, no. 2: 219–31.

Andrijasevic, Rutvica, and Devi Sacchetto. 2017. "'Disappearing Workers': Foxconn in Europe and the Changing Role of Temporary Work Agencies." *Work, Employment and Society* 31, no. 1: 54–70.

Aneesh, Aneesh. 2006. *Virtual Migration: The Programming of Globalization.* Durham, N.C.: Duke University Press.

Aneesh, Aneesh. 2009. "Global Labour: Algocratic Modes of Organization." *Sociological Theory* 27, no. 4: 347–70.

Azmeh, Shamel, and Khalid Nadvi. 2014. "Asian Firms and the Restructuring of Global Value Chains." *International Business Review* 23, no. 4: 708–17. https://doi.org/10 .1016/j.ibusrev.2014.03.007.

Bair, Jennifer, and Matthew C. Mahutga. 2012. "Varieties of Offshoring? Spatial Fragmentation and the Organization of Production in Twenty-First Century Capitalism " In *Capitalisms and Capitalism in the Twenty-First Century,* ed. Glenn Morgan and Richard Whitley, 270–97. Oxford: Oxford University Press.

Bao, Weihong. 2015. *Fiery Cinema: The Emergence of an Affective Medium in China, 1915-1945.* Minneapolis: University of Minnesota Press.

Barrientos, Stephanie Ware. 2013. "'Labour Chains': Analysing the Role of Labour Contractors in Global Production Networks." *Journal of Development Studies* 49, no. 8: 1058–71. https://doi.org/10.1080/00220388.2013.780040.

Berntsen, Lisa, and Nathan Lillie. 2016. "Hyper-mobile Migrant Workers and Dutch Trade Union Representation Strategies at the Eemshaven Construction Sites." *Economic and Industrial Democracy* 37, no. 1: 171–87. https://doi.org/10.1177/ 0143831x14537357.

Beyes, Timon, Lisa Conrad, and Reinhold Martin. 2019. *Organize.* Minnesota: University of Minnesota Press and meson press.

Beyes, Timon, Robin Holt, and Claus Pias. 2019. *The Oxford Handbook of Media, Technology, and Organization Studies.* Oxford: Oxford University Press.

Chen, Julie Yujie. 2018. "Thrown under the Bus and Outrunning It! The Logic of Didi and Taxi Drivers' Labour and Activism in the On-Demand Economy." 20, no. 8: 2691–711.

Chen, Julie Yujie. 2020. "The Mirage and Politics of Participation in China's Platform Economy." *Javnost—The Public* 27, no. 2: 154–70. https://doi.org/10.1080/1318322 2.2020.1727271.

Chen, Julie Yujie, and Jack Linchuan Qiu. 2019. "Digital Utility: Datafication, Regulation, Labor, and DiDi's Platformization of Urban Transport in China." *Chinese Journal of Communication* 12, no. 3: 274–89. https://doi.org/10.1080/17544750.2019.161 4964.

Chen, Julie Yujie, and Ping Sun. 2020. "Temporal Arbitrage, the Fragmented Rush, and Opportunistic Behaviors: The Labor Politics of Time in the Platform Economy." *New Media & Society.* https://doi.org/https://doi.org/10.1177/1461444820913567.

Coe, Neil M., Martin Hess, Henry Wai-chung Yeung, Peter Dicken, and Jeffrey Henderson. 2004. "'Globalizing' Regional Development: A Global Production Networks Perspective." *Transactions of the Institute of British Geographers* 29, no. 4: 468–84.

Coe, Neil M., Katharine Jones, and Kevin Ward. 2010. "The Business of Temporary Staffing: A Developing Research Agenda." *Geography Compass* 4, no. 8: 1055–68.

Cowen, Deborah. 2014. *The Deadly Life of Logistics: Mapping Violence in Global Trade.* Minneapolis: University of Minnesota Press.

CzechFocus. 2007. "Interview with Jim Chang, General Manager of Foxconn CZ." *Translation from Hospodarske Noviny, 10 April 2007.* Accessed June 20, 2013. http://www .czechinvest.org/data/files/cf-2-2007-603.pdf.

Doane, Mary Ann. 2016."Information, Crisis, Catastrophe." In *New Media, Old Media : A History and Theory Reader,* 2nd ed., ed. Wendy Hui Kyong Chun, Anna Watkins Fisher, and Thomas Keenan, 307–21. New York: Routledge.

Elson, Diane, and Ruth Pearson. 1981. "'Nimble Fingers Make Cheap Workers': An Analysis of Women's Employment in Third World Export Manufacturing." *Feminist review* 7, no. 1: 87–107.

Evans, David S., and Richard Schmalensee. 2016. *Matchmakers: The New Economics of Multisided Platforms.* Boston, Mass.: Harvard Business Review Press.

Galloway, Alex. 2001. "Protocol, or, How Control Exists after Decentralization." *Rethinking Marxism* 13, no. 3: 81–88.

Gandini, Alessandro. 2019. "Labour Process Theory and the Gig Economy." *Human Relations* 72, no. 6: 1039–56.

Gordon, Jennifer. 2017. "Regulating the Human Supply Chain." *Iowa Law Review* 102, no. 445: 445–503.

Gottfried, H. 1992. "In the Margins: Flexibility as a Mode of Regulation in the Temporary Help Service Industry." *Work, Employment & Society* 6, no. 4: 443–60.

Graham, Mark, Isis Hjorth, and Vili Lehdonvirta. 2017. "Digital Labour and Development: Impacts of Global Digital Labour Platforms and the Gig Economy on Worker Livelihoods." *Transfer: European Review of Labour and Research* 23, no. 2: 135–62.

Grappi, Giorgio. 2020. "L'ordine logistico come problema politico, tra esperienze storiche di cibernetica per il socialismo e la piattaforma come piano." *Quaderni di Scienza & Politica* 8:331–56.

Gregg, Melissa. 2011. *Work's Intimacy.* Cambridge: Polity.

Gregg, Melissa. 2018. *Counterproductive: Time Management in the Knowledge Economy.* Durham, N.C.: Duke University Press.

Hayes, Lydia, and Tonia Novitz. 2013. "Workers without Footprints: The Legal Fiction of Migrant Workers as Posted Workers." In *Labour Migration in Hard Times: Reforming Labour Market Regulation:* ed. Bernard Ryan, 99–118. Liverpool: Institute of Employment Rights, London.

Holl, Adelheid, Rafael Pardo, and Ruth Rama. 2009. "Just-in-Time Manufacturing Systems, Subcontracting, and Geographic Proximity." *Regional Studies* 44, no. 5: 519–33. https://doi.org/10.1080/00343400902821626.

Hope, Wayne. 2006. "Global Capitalism and the Critique of Real Time." *Time & Society* 15, no. 2–3: 275–302. https://doi.org/10.1177/0961463x06066943.

Hope, Wayne. 2009. "Conflicting Temporalities." *Time & Society* 18, no. 1: 62–85. https://doi.org/10.1177/0961463x08099943.

Hope, Wayne. 2016. *Time, Communication, and Global Capitalism.* International Political Economy Series. Basingstoke, UK: Palgrave MacMillan.

Howe, Joanna, and Rosemary Owens. 2016. "Temporary Labour Migration in the Global Era: The Regulatory Challenges." In *Temporary Labour Migration in the Global Era,* ed. Joanna Howe and Rosemary Owens, 3–40. Oñati International Series in Law and Society. Oxford, UK: Hart Publishing.

Huws, Ursula, Neil Spenser, Matthew Coates, and Kaire Holts. 2019. *The Platformization of Work in Europe: Results from Research in 13 European Countries.* Brussels: Foundation for European Progressive Studies. https://uhra.herts.ac.uk/bitstream/handle/2299/21638/the_platformisation_of_work_in_europe_final_corrected.pdf?sequence=1.

Hyman, Louis. 2018. *Temp: How American Work, American Business, and the American Dream Became Temporary.* New York: Viking.

Irani, Lilly. 2015. "Difference and Dependence among Digital Workers: The Case of Amazon Mechanical Turk." *South Atlantic Quarterly* 114, no. 1: 225–34.

Jenkins, Jean, and Paul Blyton. 2017. "In Debt to the Time-Bank: The Manipulation of Working Time in Indian Garment Factories and 'Working Dead Horse.'" *Work, Employment & Society* 31, no. 1: 90–105. https://doi.org/10.1177/0950017016664679.

Kenney, Martin, and Richard Florida. 1988. "Beyond Mass Production: Production and the Labor Process in Japan." *Politics & Society* 16, no. 1: 121–58.

LeBaron, Genevieve, and Nicola Phillips. 2018. "States and the Political Economy of Unfree Labour." *New Political Economy* 24, no. 1: 1–21. https://doi.org/10.1080/13563467.2017.1420642.

Lee, Ching Kwan. 1995. "Engendering the Worlds of Labor: Women Workers, Labor Markets, and Production Politics in the South China Economic Miracle." *American Sociological Review* 60, no. 3: 378–97.

Lüthje, Boy, Stefanie Hürtgen, Peter Pawlicki, and Martina Sproll. 2013. *From Silicon Valley to Shenzhen: Global Production and Work in the IT Industry.* Washington, D.C.: Rowman & Littlefield.

Mussche, Ninke, and Dries Lens. 2018. "The EU Free Movement of Services and the Growing Mobility of Third-Country Nationals as Posted Workers." University of Antwerp Herman Deleeck Centre for Social Policy, Antwerpen, Belgium. https://medialibrary.uantwerpen.be/oldcontent/container2453/files/CSB%20WP%202018/CSBWorkingPaper1813.pdf

Nadeem, Shehzad. 2009. "The Uses and Abuses of Time: Globalization and Time Arbitrage in India's Outsourcing Industries." *Global Networks* 9, no. 1: 20–40.

Nishimoto, Ikuko. 2002. "Cooperation Engineered: Efficiency in the 'Just-in-Time' Systems." In *Making Time: Time and Management in Modern Organizations,* ed. Richard Whipp, Barbara Adam, and Ida Sabelis, 104–14. Oxford: Oxford University Press.

Novitz, Tonia, and Rutvica Andrijasevic. 2020. "Reform of the Posting of Workers Regime—An Assessment of the Practical Impact on Unfree Labour Relations." *JCMS: Journal of Common Market Studies* 58, no. 5: 1325–41.

Pawlicki, Peter. 2017. *Challenger Multinationals in Telecommunications: Huawei and ZTE.* Brussels: ETUI.

Poster, Winifred Rebecca. 2007. "Saying 'Good Morning' in the Night: The Reversal of Work Time in Global ICT Service Work." *Workplace Temporalities: Research in Sociology of Work* 17:55–112.

Prassl, Jeremias, and Martin Risak. 2015. "Uber, Taskrabbit, and Co.: Platforms as Employers? Rethinking the Legal Analysis of Crowdwork." *Comparative Labor Law & Policy Journal* 37:619.

Pun, Ngai. 2007. "Gendering the Dormitory Labor System: Production, Reproduction, and Migrant Labor in South China." *Feminist Economics* 13, no. 3–4: 239–58.

Pun, Ngai, Rutvica Andrijasevic, and Devi Sacchetto. 2020. "Transgressing North–South Divide: Foxconn Production Regimes in China and the Czech Republic." *Critical Sociology* 46, no. 2: 307–22.

Purser , E. Ronald. 2002. "Contested Present: Critical Perspectives on 'Real-time' Management." In *Making Time: Time and Management in Modern Organizations,* ed. Richard Whipp, Barbara Adam and Ida Sabelis, 155–67. Oxford: Oxford University Press.

Qiu, Jack Linchuan. 2017. *Goodbye iSlave: A Manifesto for Digital Abolition.* Champaign: University of Illinois Press.

Qiu, Jack Linchuan, Melissa Gregg, and Kate Crawford. 2014. "Circuits of Labour: A Labour Theory of the iPhone Era." *tripleC* 12, no. 2: 564–81.

Rochet, Jean-Charles, and Jean Tirole. 2003. "Platform Competition in Two-Sided Markets." *Journal of the European Economic Association* 1, no. 4: 990–1029.

Sayer, Andrew. 1986. "New Developments in Manufacturing: The Just-in-Time System." *Capital & Class* 10, no. 3: 43–72.

Sharma, Sarah. 2017a. "Exit and the Extension of Man." *Transmediale.* https://archive.transmediale.de/content/exit-and-the-extensions-of-man.

Sharma, Sarah. 2017b. "Speed Traps and the Temporal: Of Taxis, Truck Stops, and

TaskRabbits." In *The Sociology of Speed: Digital, Organizational, and Social Temporalities,* ed. Judy Wajcman and Nigel Dodd, 131–51. Oxford: Oxford University Press.

Smith, Chris. 2003. "Living at Work: Management Control and the Dormitory Labour System in China." *Asia Pacific Journal of Management* 20, no. 3: 333–58. https://doi.org/10.1023/a:1024097432726.

Steinberg, Marc. 2019. *The Platform Economy: How Japan Transformed the Consumer Internet.* Minneapolis: University of Minnesota Press.

Steinberg, Marc. Forthcoming. "From Automobile Capitalism to Platform Capitalism: Toyotism as a Prehistory of Digital Platforms." *Organization Studies.*

Taylor, Bill W. K. 2006. "A Feminist Critique of Japanization: Employment and Work in Consumer Electronics." *Gender, Work and Organization* 13, no. 4: 317–37.

Theodore, Nik, and Jamie Peck. 2002. "The Temporary Staffing Industry: Growth Imeratives and Limits of Contingency." *Economic Geography* 78, no. 4: 463–93.

Thomas, Llewellyn D. W., Erkko Autio, and David M. Gann. 2014. "Architectural Leverage: Putting Platforms in Context." *Academy of management perspectives* 28, no. 2: 198–219.

Thommes, Kirsten, and Katrin Weiland. 2010. "Explanatory Factors for Firms' Use of Temporary Agency Work in Germany." *European Management Journal* 28, no. 1: 55–67.

Tsing, Anna. 2009. "Supply Chain and the Human Condition." *Rethinking Marxism* 21, no. 2: 148–76.

van Doorn, Niels. 2017. "Platform Labor: On the Gendered and Racialized Exploitation of Low-Income Service Work in the 'On-Demand' Economy." *Information, Communication & Society* 20, no. 6: 898–914. https://doi.org/10.1080/1369118x.2017.129 4194.

Wajcman, Judy. 2019a. "The Digital Architecture of Time Management." *Science, Technology, & Human Values* 44, no. 2: 315–37. https://doi.org/10.1177/016224391879 5041.

Wajcman, Judy. 2019b. "How Silicon Valley Sets Time." *New Media & Society* 21, no. 6: 1272–89.

Wajcman, Judy, and Nigel Dodd. 2017. *The Sociology of Speed: Digital, Organizational, and Social Temporalities.* Oxford: Oxford University Press.

Xiang Biao. 2007. *Global "Body Shopping": An Indian Labor System in the Information Technology Industry.* Princeton, N.J.: Princeton University Press.

Xiang Biao and, Johan Lindquist. 2014. "Migration Infrastructure." *International Migration Review* 48, no. 1: 122–48.

Yamada, Masahiko. 2010. "The Current Issues on Foreign Workers in Japan." *Japan Labour Review* 7, no. 3: 5–18.

3

Spaces of Labor Mediation: Policy, Platform, and Media

Julie Yujie Chen

When it comes to the organization of work in capitalism, management and media almost always intertwine. Workers are managed by the invention and deployment of technological and ideological systems that not only monitor and evaluate workers' output at the workplace but shape the normative perception and anticipation of work in society (Gregg 2011). For some, media is a formidable ordering force of technology throughout history that has transformed the construction of self, collective, and social realities (Couldry and Hepp 2016). For others, the managerial shift for enterprises to minimize the employment liability and eventually to define a stable work force as a liability (Hyman 2018) is an overlooked force that precipitated the flexibilization of production in developed societies post–World War II. The ascendency of managerialism as a new social order (Boltanski and Chiapello 2007; Shatil 2020), as Shatil points out, represents a diffusion of the managerial logic outside of the workplace and an alignment with "the interests, values and discourses of managerial dominance" (2020, 2). The achievement of such an alignment cannot be fully understood without interrogating the construction of the exemplary neoliberal citizen as a worker who is agile (or flexible), creative, entrepreneurial, and productive

(Gregg 2018; Irani 2019; Boltanski and Chiapello 2007). The question of how a model working subject is constructed, circulated, and contested, however, may lead one to the fields of media and cultural studies for more inspiration. The line of inquiry seems circular. The intellectual cross-fertilization with management theory may generate new insights about the terms and conditions of work, especially when media scholars start arguing that media ought to be understood "as a constellation that organizes the production of life and labor" (Zehle and Rossiter 2015).

Management studies and media studies, and their respective sub- or related fields, find common interests in examining companies like Amazon, Facebook, Microsoft, and Toyota as platforms. But the question of how management theory may have informed the conception and operation of the platform has not yet generated much constructive inquiry in the field of media studies. In an exceptional examination of Japanese management literature and the mobile internet industry, Steinberg (2019) rightfully pinpoints the absence of Japanese platform theory, which dates back to 1994, in the intellectual historicization of platform studies, a field that is dominated by the Anglophone experience and epistemic paradigms.[1] Inserting Japanese experience and management literature in the genealogy of platform theory not only does justice to the "prehistory of the platform as we know it" (Steinberg 2019, 25), but points to a pathway to engage with management theory of the platform as a mediation process and think media through a management point of view (Steinberg 2019, 3–9).

Focusing on Chinese digital platforms, this chapter examines the intersections of management and mediation of labor in the so-called platform economy. I argue that the terms of mediation for labor management are implicated in the discourses and practices of management at different scales and in varied and precarious organizational shapes, which I call spaces of labor mediation. The spatial lens is flexible enough to allow me to explore and connect three seemingly discrete domains where labor management are mediated, practically and discursively. Namely, they are national policies, labor process control and management practices, and mass media representation. These different layers and scope of management practice and technology are emblematic of the shifting terrain of labor politics in the platform economy.

In the first section, I bring in the analytical categories of state and policy (Wang 2001) to chart out the constructed new norms around platform work in China. Considering the normative construction process as managed spaces of mediation, I will show how the state's policies supply new vocabulary and aggressively shape the cognitive parameters to understand the meanings of the platform work.

Then I take the food-delivery platforms such as Ele.me and Meituan as examples and show that as the digital platform becomes a constitutive device to structure the transactions and market "encounters" (Çalışkan and Callon 2010), the labor process and management practices are obfuscated through layers of mediation by a joint effort of the platform companies and the temp staffing industry. The consequentially elusive contractual relations for workers aggravate an already precarious work force.

In the third part, I follow a cultural studies tradition to analyze the images of food-delivery workers in mass media, which evolve from hasty riders who were forced to put speed before safety to the everyday worker hero during the coronavirus outbreak in 2020. These mediated worker images steer the public conversation away from the structural necessity to regulate the platform companies and improve work conditions and toward extolling riders' virtues and fulfilment of social responsibilities. The tendency to moralize delivery work undermines the rights-based and regulation-oriented pro-labor agenda.

Taking these three spaces of labor mediation together, I make the following two interventions. First, research on the discursive and material manifestations of labor management in the digital platform economy ought to confront the role played by policies, not just as a regulatory or geographical context but also as an active

force that shapes cultural norms and platform labor politics. This
entails approaching regulatory and institutional realms as sites of
labor mediation. Second, it is crucial to interrogate the multiple yet
uneven terrains where the platform intersects with the existing social institutions and organizations. These terrains are where power
dynamics manifest themselves in managing the workforce and
priming workers and the public to think of the platform work from
a certain perspective. In my case study, that perspective aligns
with national priorities and corporate management rationale. This
management is also and crucially undertaken through different
forms of mediation and by media representations themselves. This
suggests that media needs to be studied as generalized spaces for
labor management.

Policy's Mediation Work: New Forms of Employment

Regulatory and policy domains are usually deemed to be outside
of conventional management studies and media studies in part
because of the tendency in the liberal democratic tradition to treat
the market, the nation-state, and the media as separate and independent spheres. In studies on Chinese media, the government's
role always occupies a central place in the analytical framework,
particularly to be examined as the institutional or instrumental
force in China's mediating between capitalism and domestic
politics since the economic reforms of the late 1970s (Hong 2017;
Zhao 2003).

Instead of treating the omnipresence of the state in the internet
sectors as merely a background (Kloet et al. 2019), I am interested
in the managerial roles played by the government via policies that
actively shape popular culture and, in this case, popular percep-
tions of platform labor. The managerial roles are most salient in
the state's changed strategy to govern public opinion. No longer
merely concerned with coercion or top-down intervention (Schneider 2018), the central government has devised a mechanism to

delegate the governance work to non-state actors like private companies to monitor, guide, and control the public opinion on the internet (Hou 2019). These non-state actors are institutionalized in the configuration of the networked environment toward mass persuasion and social discipline (Schneider 2018).

Along these lines, the government also leverages the policies to help mediate the meanings of certain social and cultural phenomena associated with work. It assumes a "pedagogical" role by introducing new vocabularies from policy documents to be circulated to the domains of knowledge production and popular culture, inventing or reinventing the "social imaginary, and with it, a new subject" (Wang 2001, 29). A past example of the pedagogical instrument is the invention and mobilization of *suzhi* (quality) to construct an ideal subject of the female migrant domestic worker and establish a linkage between their market value and their personal qualities such as civility and self-discipline (H. Yan 2003).

The disciplinary and pedagogical nudge via policies and official documents, complementing the direct control by the central government, helps to achieve certain forms of cultural hegemony. As Wang (2001) argues, following Gramsci, "[common] sense as new means of enculturation [is] the key to hegemony" (2001, 43). Cultural hegemony thus contributes to naturalizing the ruling technology of the central government (Wang 2001).

A new vocabulary introduced to shape the common sense around platform work in China is the term "new forms of employment." The term first appeared in the official lexicon in the Communiqué of the Fifth Plenary Session of the 18th Central Committee of the CPC in 2015 (*Xinhua News Agency* 2015), and then was used in Premier Li's Report on the Work of the Government (2016). In April 2017, the State Council issued *Opinions on Efforts Relating to Employment and Entrepreneurship for the Moment and Near Future,* which dedicated one section of two guiding policy items on how to "support the development of new forms of employment" (State Council 2017).

The term "new forms of employment" is rendered strategically
vague and aspirational in official policy documents. On one hand,
the ambiguity of the term is designed to invite various social actors
to discuss and negotiate its meanings. On the other hand, the
meanings constructed around newness are largely circumscribed
by the official documents and policies that are characterized by the
aspiration toward digital technology–driven development.

The policy documents, as well as several subsequent academic and
trade publications, tend to associate the newness with the digital
economy, particularly in the internet-mediated service sectors.
*Opinions on Efforts Relating to Employment and Entrepreneurship
for the Moment and Near Future,* for instance, singled out flexibility
as the main characteristic of "new forms of employment" (State
Council 2017). Apart from that, there were no definitive criteria for
the "new forms of employment," of which the scope may include
any type of employment, from gig to entrepreneurial to freelancing
work, as long as the work is performed in a digitally mediated
environment.

In spite and because of the strategic vagueness, in 2017, the term
"new forms of employment" was quickly picked up by members
of the National People's Congress and scholars. Shortly after, it
entered the public domain through official documents, policies,
and academic publications, which in turn has lent cultural impetus
to the term. For example, *Reports on China's Population and Labor,*
published annually by the Social Science Academic Press, is an
authoritative report series edited by leading academics in the fields
of demographics, economics, labor and employment, and social
security. Prior to 2017, the annual report was typically structured
around key policy changes happening in the previous year, such
as the lift of the One-Child Policy, and thematized articles on the
employment structure, income gap, poverty, and the social security
system. In 2017, it started new sections on the "new economy" and
"new jobs." Ever since, the *Reports* series has at least one section
dedicated to articles on the new economy, new employment, the
new labor market, and so on.

The vagueness of the term invites scholars to discuss the conceptual definitions of the term. For example, Zhang Chenggang, a lecturer on labor economics at Capital University of Economics and Business who wrote a book on the topic, defines new forms of employment as "activities to acquire income by a workforce that is mobilized by technological innovation such as e-commerce or online platforms" (Zhang 2019, 9). As the key criterion for this definition is workers in the sectors associated with "technological innovation," he singles out three exemplary new forms of employment: (1) workers or entrepreneurs in an e-commerce platform ecology such as Alibaba's; (2) worker-partners in the two- or multi-sided platform-mediated markets such as drivers on ride-hailing platforms; and (3) workers on crowdwork platforms (Zhang 2019). Other scholars define the term by the characteristics of flexibility, nonstandard contracts, de-institutionalization of employment, and platformization (G. Xiao 2019). Shen Manhong, the president of Ningbo University, singled out four aspects of newness in "the new forms of employment" for college graduates: (1) new sectors like e-commerce and the sharing economy; (2) new employment relations that are established with internet platforms rather than the traditional "work unit" *(danwei)*;[2] (3) new opportunities for entrepreneurship; and (4) new notions of flexible work and multiple part-time jobs (*People's Daily 2018*).

Leading platform companies also published research reports, adopting the language of government policy, to advocate "the new forms of employment." For example, the ride-hailing platform company DiDi Chuxing published a report entitled *New Economy, New Jobs* to profile drivers working on the platform (DiDi Institute of Policy Study 2017). The food-delivery platform Ele.me, now a subsidiary of the e-commerce giant Alibaba, published a report on its riders, calling them "new youth" with "new occupation" and "new values" (Ele.me 2020). The report also describes 56 percent of the riders who work a second job as "slashie youth" and normalizes having "(multiple) second jobs" as a new signature lifestyle of this generation (Ele.me 2020).[3] No distinction was made between the privilege to choose a "slashie" lifestyle and the necessity to work multiple jobs to make ends meet, which has everything to do with social inequality.

The mediation for the meanings of "the new forms of employment" is not always celebratory, but open for cautious and critical voices. Several scholars point to the labor exploitation and the reinforcement of inequality in the platform economy (J. Y. Chen 2018; Wen 2018). The advocates of new forms of employment also acknowledge the regulatory loopholes that need to be fixed in order to protect workers and govern platform companies (Zhang 2019). A member of the CPPCC National Committee—a political legislative advisory body in China that participates in making important national-level political decisions—urged lawmakers to develop a more precise definition of the new forms of employment and then to initiate corresponding social security reforms (G. Xiao 2019). Several municipal governments and local trade union branches have initiated social security reforms for flexible workers (Zhang 2019).

Despite these voices of caution, the knowledge produced by pro-government scholars to understand the newness is largely affirmative about the state's priority to "digitize" and upgrade the economy and transform workers' skills to "digital skills" (Zhang 2019). This suggests scholars are embracing the managerial and pedagogical rationale of the government. In China, as elsewhere, the digital economy is mystified to be a more advanced stage of development toward which developing countries aspire. Information technologies have been a great source of social imagination for the public in China since the 1980s (Liu 2019). State policies, like development plans, are crucial texts to reframe economic development as a question of innovation to which digital technologies are the primary solution (Irani 2019; Hong 2017). The discursive currency of the term "new forms of employment" accentuates the aspirational aspect (Duffy 2016) of working in the digital economy. When associated with the national development agenda, the aspirational labor of individual workers is also nudged toward aligning with the developmental priorities of the nation-state.

Moreover, the "new forms of employment" is made into a floating signifier and mobilized to erase the historical precariousness of Chinese informal work and produce new norms around working in the digital economy. Nonstandard contracts and unstable jobs, hardly anything categorically new to the platform economy, have been the norm for a majority of Chinese workers since China's economic reform in the late 1970s (Lee and Kofman 2012). The persistence of informal employment is part of state design in many developing countries driven by developmentalism (Lee and Kofman 2012), which makes it challenging to interrogate the impact of flexible capitalism or the digital economy on Chinese workers.

The floating signifier is insufficient to lift the structural barriers facing informal workers in real life, which undermines the progressive policy reforms. The aforementioned "Opinions on Efforts Relating to Employment and Entrepreneurship for the Moment and Near Future" (hereafter "Efforts Relating to Employment") encouraged the construction of an "online social security [platform]" so that "flexible" workers can participate in the social security programs more easily and make their benefits "transferable". It stressed the responsibilities of platform companies for contributing to the social security accounts of those workers who are under labor contracts with the platform companies. However, it ignored the reality that the booming platform economy is dominated by informal workers who had limited collective bargaining power and most of whom had no labor contracts (J. Y. Chen 2018; Sun 2019; Zhang 2019). China's 2008 Labor Contract Law only guarantees labor protection and access to the associated social security, health insurance, and welfare to workers who sign and obtain a formal and legal labor contract. Therefore, the solution envisioned in the "Efforts Relating to Employment" to expand the social security programs to platform workers is unlikely to produce concrete benefits for workers if the structural barriers preventing them from obtaining labor contracts persist. Theoretically speaking, when there is no labor contract, workers can still resort to the judiciary system to pass judgment on an effective employment relationship that would hold the employers accountable. However, in practice, only a fraction of the cases of labor disputes in the platform economy were ruled in favor of workers where no labor contracts were offered (Zhang 2019).

In short, policy's mediation of labor, via the term "new forms of employment," naturalizes contingent employment and structural inequalities in the platform economy. By proactively repackaging the longstanding precariousness and informal employment as conditions for a future-oriented digital development agenda, the central government and its policies sanction and reinforce platform companies' management and organizational logic that projects the "mirage" of a platform-enabled participatory environment for workers (J. Y. Chen 2020). Furthermore, the ambiguity of the term is designed to invite various social actors to define and negotiate its meanings but only within the parameter of the aspirational discourse set by the official documents. This kind of mediation dovetails with the government's management strategy in other areas such as public opinions on the internet (Schneider 2018). Because of the embrace of digital developmentalism, the process of meaning making and negations of the term "new forms of employment" by scholars, private companies, and local courts functions as what Bolatanski and Chiapello (2007) call "justificatory operations" to generate more legitimacy for the term "new forms of employment." This legitimacy in turn contributes to producing the hegemonic imaginary and new norms of platform work in the broad context of the platformization of work and management of the workforce.

Platform and Outsourcing: Mediation of Labor, Management of the Workforce

Policy's mediation of labor in constructing normative working behaviors helps obscure the real transformations to the practices of labor management in the platform economy. In this section, I use food-delivery services in China as a point of departure to examine the intermediary and mediatory role played by the temp staffing industry and the platforms in assembling, disassembling, and managing the workforce. This focus on the ways in which digital platforms intersect with temp staffing agencies in shaping the organization of work and the labor process dispel the mirage of platform-enabled participatory environment for workers and brings into view the real transformations to the management practices and labor politics. New forms of precarity arise from platform companies' dynamic deployment of their technological apparatuses of management (e.g. algorithms) and labor outsourcing via temp staffing agencies.

The metaphor of the ecosystem, which is rooted in the historical conceptions of platforms as business models in management studies in 1990s, is useful to comprehend the management thinking in the platform economy, including the platform-mediated food-delivery services in China. Different from the platform models that are concerned with the organizational form and the intermediary position of the firm (Rochet and Tirole 2003; Thomas et al. 2014), the platform ecosystem model assumes that a product or company can only succeed based on the existence (and success) of its complementors (see van Dijck, Poell, and Waal 2018). This inspires a paradigm shift in management thinking, which requires firms to adopt the strategy to achieve market dominance in the business ecology, or even to create a new business ecology if needed (Kenney and Zysman 2016; J. Moore 1993). The priority to achieve scale is the common mantra for platform companies from Amazon and Uber to Ele.me and Meituan, the last two being the market leaders in food-delivery services in China.

For the digital platform, mediation is the key element in the management apparatus to construct the ecosystem wherein the platform reconfigures the industrial dynamic and creates new forms of competition and collaboration in the market (Gawer 2011; J. Moore 1993). The creation of both the ecosystem and the market, far from being natural or smooth, involves much capital investment and sociotechnical power to capture real-time information about customer demand and the pool of available riders, to allocate jobs, to design delivery routes, to set prices, and so on. Many scholars from both management studies and media studies contend that digital platforms are a new social ordering force because their computational or algorithmic power that allows actions to be taken automatically across multiple scales and domains (Kenney and Zysman 2016) and the data power at a company's disposal (van Dijck, Poell, and Waal 2018).

In addition to technological reconfigurations, equally important but less discussed are the management innovations implemented by digital platforms. As Langley and Leyson (2017, 3) pointed out, following Çalışkan and Callon's idea of marketization (2010), the logic of platform intermediation is "to structure market encounters in the digital space." It entails dynamic management to not only mediate and sustain market encounters that are permeated with digital circulations of content, data, labor, and transactions, but also contribute to ultimately achieving market dominance.

(Re)Assembling the Labor Force

The dynamic management of markets involves changing the media or organizational form of management practices. Specifically related to labor management, two essential instruments are mobilized together by Chinese food-delivery platforms, one concerning the information asymmetries and the other concerning the dynamic deployment of management organizations and technologies specifically related to the wage system and labor contracts. Together, the two instruments help form what I call the dynamic (re)assembly of the labor force. The management technique of (re)assembling the labor force based primarily on the platform's strategic and contextual needs is what sets the platform management of labor apart and what engenders intensified precarity.

In the food-delivery platform ecosystem, the platform company is the only player that has all the information about the constructed market, which constitutes an asymmetrical relation between the platform and other parties (Rosenblat and Stark 2016). This information asymmetry gives the platform a panoramic view of the market, such that it is well positioned to intervene in its own interests. This intervention is manual as much as it is algorithmic.

As a principal engineer at one of leading food-delivery platform companies explained in an interview,

> We have a real-time surveillance system. . . . Since job allocation is completed automatically [*sic*], we need such a system to monitor . . . [and] watch over the workings of our platform in all business districts across the city on one hand. On the other hand, we can intervene manually if something goes wrong. (Engineer A)[4]

When I asked him to give me an example of a "manual intervention," he spoke of transferring the pool of outstanding orders from riders who are not restricted by distance to the location-bounded riders if the orders stay unclaimed for too long.

In the Beijing food-delivery service sector, there are at least four types of riders: (1) platform-hired riders, (2) crowdsourced riders (i.e., self-employed), (3) outsourced/subcontracted riders, and (4) in-house riders hired by the restaurants (Figure 1).[5] These riders differ in their contractual relationship, collective bargaining power, and also in both pay schemes and benefits. The heterogeneous riders are also managed differently along the development of the platform (Figure 2). The variety of riders and management structures existing today are a deliberate invention by platform companies. They are emblematic of the dynamic ways in which platform companies mobilize technologies, existing informal economic structures, and management practices to meet their goals of labor force regulation at different stages of development. Leading food-delivery platforms in China, founded over a period of five years, from 2009 to 2014,[6] all started their services by hiring and managing riders directly. Gradually they moved to incorporate crowdsourced riders as independent contractors for the platform, and then the remaining platforms on the market started to adopt an outsourced model of delivery service, adding temp staffing agencies to their labor management structures while the number of platform-hired riders was on decline (Figure 2).

As far as the platform-mediated work environment is concerned, only crowdsourced riders face no distance restrictions on the orders they can take, while other types of riders usually work within specific business districts or neighborhoods with a roughly three-kilometer radius. Contrary to the popular myth of the nonhuman algorithmic boss (Rosenblat and Stark 2016), all riders except the crowdsourced ones are managed through a local office (known as a team or station). I will return to the relationship between the local office and the platform later. In the local management office, which is typically equipped with several desktop computers, human intervention is common. On the interactive maps shown

Types of riders	Employer	Labor contract	Base salary	Social security contributions	Pay system
Platform-hired	Platform company	Yes	Yes	Platform and individual	Piece rate pay, benefits, bonus, and incentives
Crowdsourced	Self-employed	No	No	No	Dynamic rate pay and incentives
Outsourced	Third-party staffing agencies	Mostly no	Mostly no	It depends	Piece rate pay and incentives
In-house	Restaurant	Mostly no	Mostly no	It depends	It depends

[Figure 3.1]. Different types of food-delivery riders and their respective labor rights.

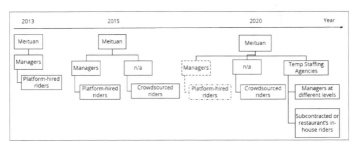

[Figure 3.2]. Evolving management structures of riders in the platform system (the example of Meituan).

on the computer screen, the manager (known as the team/station leader or *zhanzhang*) monitors the riders' real-time performance in the area. With one click, the manager can see an individual rider's detailed performance history. If needed, the manager could, for example, transfer the incoming orders from a rider who is behind schedule, overwriting the initial algorithmic allocation to said rider, to another less busy rider in the area. As one station leader explained, the survival and prosperity of his station depends on the "stats" that can prove the efficiency and completion of orders in the covered area.

In the manual interventions made by the platform's engineering team to mobilize the crowdsourced and outsourced riders, the operation of asymmetric information power is intended to incentivize labor supply in business districts where local team leaders are responsible. But the local team of riders and their managers are kept in the dark. In practice, other technologies of management such as changing the incentives or wage schemes are used along with this technique to shift the market for different types of riders, especially to attract new workers or to reduce the cost of veteran workers. Financial incentives like dynamic pricing and rewards are popular management strategies in digital platform design. By leveraging financial incentives, platforms are believed to be able to "staff the right number of on-demand workers at the right time" (Allon, Cohen, and Sinchaisri 2018, 2). Between 2016 and early 2017, platform-hired food-delivery riders enjoyed a brief period of decent wages and generous incentives, bonuses, and rewards, partially because of the fierce competition between platforms to attract workers. For instance, Zhu was an Ele.me delivery worker. He recollected a "hefty wage" of about ¥10,000 ($1,455) a month in 2017, including a base salary. "Generous" reward schemes enabled his coworker Zou to earn "¥1,000 ($146) extra every month just for the rewards from favorable customer ratings."[7]

With depleting capital reserves, the platform company Ele.me quickly shrank the financial incentives and translated the reductions into a technological configuration of the labor process. Zou

found himself frustrated by the customer rating system and the
plummeting rewards:

> At the end of last year [2017], the customer rating system
> [algorithm] changed to three smiley faces. The middle
> one is selected by default to indicate satisfaction. But we
> [the riders] need the customer to also select the right
> smiley face, because that one means "a good rating for
> the rider." I used to send SMS to customers to remind
> them of clicking the right smiley face. But then the system
> changed again. Customers needed to put in their ratings
> for "dispatching service." Then I couldn't keep up with [the
> change by] reminding all customers . . . now I only get
> about thirty favorable rates worth ¥60 ($9).

This shows that management and its business strategies, instead of
algorithms, drive the shifting conditions for platform workers. Indeed, as Moore and Joyce (2019) point out, arbitrary changes to the
pay system (violations of contractual terms) or the unstable wage
and lack of collective bargaining power are common in the history
of labor management, and also in the informal employment in
China (F. Xu 2013). Algorithms do not add anything radically new to
the existing unfair management techniques. The distinction of the
platform mediation of labor management, however, lies in the wide
range of management technologies and practices at the disposal
of the platform company and its capacity to flexibly assemble,
disassemble, and reassemble them to form, as Moore and Joyce
summarize, a management "portfolio according to the contextual
requirements" (2019, 5).

As migrant workers from rural areas account for a great majority of
food-delivery work force in the cities (Meituan Dianping 2018; Ele.
me 2020), their contractual status is correlated to their precarious
status, the level of collective-bargaining power, and the different
pay systems (Figure 1). The contractual labor relationships and
the flow of labor are managed by intermediaries: temporary work
agencies or intermediary staffing agencies. These temp staffing

agencies (TSAs) call themselves agents (*daili*) or business alliances (*jiamengshang*), but many of our informants simply refer to them as "the third-party." As Andrijasevic demonstrates in chapter 2 of this book, TSAs operate as intermediaries between workers and factories. By assuming increasing responsibility for labor management, temporary work agencies have a direct impact on the work conditions for workers (see also Andrijasevic and Sacchetto 2017). In the course of food-delivery platform development, layers of (Inter)mediation of labor contractual relations occur in the surging presence of intermediary temporary staffing agencies to help recruit and manage outsourced and restaurant in-house riders (Figures 1 and 2). Riders are increasingly organized in teams or stations in local business districts or neighborhoods. Accompanying this expansion of temp staffing agencies is the casualization and decrease of platform-hired employment and the rise of crowdsourced, outsourced, and subcontracted riders (Figure 2). As of December 2020, platform-hired riders had almost disappeared on both Ele.me and Meituan.

According to Zhu and his coworkers, their overall job quality, including income, has seen a dramatic decline as the market came under the control of two leading companies—Ele.me and Meituan in 2017, when both platforms decided to outsource their delivery services to temp staffing agencies. The wave of outsourcing that started in Beijing in late 2017 further proves that the initial hefty wages and labor protections offered by the platforms to their own riders are the ephemeral exceptions rather than the norm. From 2018 to 2019 in Beijing alone, Meituan and Ele.me worked with more than thirty temp staffing agencies to amass a labor pool, manage the workers, and shift the composition of the work force.[8]

Accompanying the wave of labor outsourcing are deteriorating work conditions and generalized precarity. In April 2018, Meituan-hired riders faced unilateral terminations of their contracts and bulk transfer of their employment relations to several different temp staffing agencies. After a three-month grace period, they lost their base salaries, labor contracts, and all of their employment benefits. They were also subjected to harsh management by the staffing company who employed them. Qi, a rider, described the transition thus:

> Now it's like we are all sold to the third party [staffing company]. You have nothing to do with Meituan from now on; the [staffing] company will take over . . . [It] will stop paying our social security and pension; there is no minimum wage. It increases our rate per delivery instead.

Qi could belong to the category of "new forms of employment" as envisioned by official government policy documents explored in the first section, and yet the unilateral termination of his labor contract shows the platform companies' strategy to regulate the work force by manipulating contractual relations and pay systems (Figure 1). Qi felt ambivalent about the increased piece rate as he could earn "more income" if he maintained the volume of deliveries but, without a minimum wage, the income stream was "less stable." Several of Qi's coworkers quit in protest against Meituan's decision, but others including Qi stayed and became outsourced riders.

Subcontracted riders, usually working full time on a fixed schedule, face compounded management and control from the platform and the temp staffing agency, similar to the manufacturing workers in Rutvica Andrijasevic's chapter in this volume. The platform company designs and implements all the algorithms at work (e.g., delivery time, route, rewards) and has the power to change the algorithm at will, as shown in its mobilization of crowdsourced riders and the unpredictable rewarding algorithms experienced by Zhu. The platform is also able to shift its contracting terms with temp staffing agencies, encouraging them to compete against each other and leverage the available supply of crowdsourced riders (Figure 2). On the other hand, temp staffing agencies practice a location-based internal hierarchy of labor management. Riders are managed by station or district managers who report to their supervisors at the municipal or regional levels. Temp staffing agencies can set their own pay rate within the permitted ranges and implement various management policies of attendance, schedule, reward and punishment, and so on. For example, most subcontracted riders, and increasingly, restaurant in-house riders, are required to stay online during lunch and dinner peak times, from 11:00am to 2:00pm and 5:00 to 8:00pm. Staffing agencies usually have punitive policies for late delivery. Managers may withhold wages worth several thousand RMB in the name of a "security deposit" to intimidate workers into compliance. They can also set daily minimum quotas for deliveries. A team manager, Zhang, reported,

> We just had a new rule [in my team] which demanded everyone to complete at least eighteen orders per day. Otherwise, we don't get the perfect attendance allowance—¥800 (approx. $116).

The temp staffing agencies are set to compete against each other in the same area in a platform-controlled market in order to drive the labor cost down for the sake of a platform's competitiveness. Look no further than the thirty staffing agencies in Beijing. This is why the team manager quoted above admitted that his team depends on their "stats."

Because they have to cope with unpredictable changes to the algorithms, riders like Zou experience an intensification of labor. Along with that, the proliferation of informal work types of food-delivery riders (Figure 1) suggests a continued trend of the multiplication of labor (Mezzadra and Neilson 2013) in that the internally diversified labor force contributes to the creation of relative surplus value. As Irani (2015) argues, the differentiation of labor is the feature, not the bug, in the world of platform work. The increasing prominence of temp staffing agencies in the platform-mediated food-delivery sector is not accidental, but rather suggests the platform's capacity to exploit and thrive on the preexisting labor-management practices. The labor subcontracting systems have been used widely in manufacturing, construction, and service industries in China and other countries long before the rise of digital platforms (F. Xu 2013; Peck and Theodore 2001). The global trend of the flexibilization of the workforce has given rise to the flourishing of temp staffing agencies, many operating translocally or transnationally (Andrijasevic and Sacchetto 2017), making them an active force in restructuring the spaces of labor management. In many respects, subcontracted food-delivery riders face the same old challenges as others in the temp staffing industry: wage theft, harsh management, and lack of substantive labor protection and social security. These familiar problems defy the claims of a rise of new forms of employment as conveyed in the policies and government documents that pivot on flexibility or multiple jobs.

However, what distinguishes the platform-controlled management of the labor force is their evolving and shifting strategies that assemble and reassemble the available and potential workers and precipitate a proliferation of varied forms of informality in order to achieve market dominance and to construct a platform ecosystem. Platforms assemble and reassemble the labor force at a pace seldom seen before or in other industries. The current stage as shown in Figure 2 may give way to another combination of management models in the future. However, in the absence of regulatory interventions, the continued intersection of intermediary staffing agencies and digital platforms (which have crowdsourced riders as "the reserve army of labor") would further destabilize and obscure the managerial organization and structuring of the work force. The elusive layers of labor mediation are designed to enhance labor exploitation and intensify worker precarity, which are in the interest of capital accumulation for platform companies. A third area of labor mediation is found in the media representation of these riders, to which I now turn.

The Cultural Work of Media Representations: Between "Crazy Riders" "Trapped in the System" and Everyday Heroes

On March 19, 2020, *Time* published a special issue called "When the World Stops," featuring six cover stories that show how "regular

people around the world . . . adapt to a new reality" of the coronavirus pandemic (*Time* Staff 2020). Zhixiao Gao, a Meituan delivery
worker in Beijing, was among the six. On the *Time* website, a video
interview of Gao was posted along with the article, which followed
part of his delivery journey in a lockdown Beijing. In the video
interview, Gao described a changed feeling about the job since
"everyone is understanding and tolerant toward each other during
the outbreak" as opposed to his past experience of getting negative
reviews from unhappy customers. Completing sixty to seventy deliveries a day, he was proud that he "can make money and also help
other people" during the pandemic, Gao said in the video interview.
The *Time* article highlighted Gao taking care of an elderly female
neighbor who has diabetes (Campbell 2020). He not only took the
prescription from the woman's home and collected the requested
medication from a nearby hospital but also kept her company for
a while, cooked for her, and took out the trash when he left. "I am
just an ordinary person," Gao concluded, "People like us can make
our unsung contribution during this special period of time. Being
able to help more people is what gives me the biggest joy."[9]

The cover story on Gao generated a sweeping echo of reporting on
Chinese food-delivery workers across the state-controlled media
like *People's Daily* and *China Daily,* major internet portals like Sina
and Sohu, and other influential media and online forums like the
Paper and Zhihu. The Hong Kong–based pro-labor organization
China Labour Bulletin also posted Gao's picture on its Facebook
page. A thread running through this wave of media coverage is a
widespread recognition of food-delivery riders' work during the
pandemic. Some called them the "urban ferryman" who risk their
lives to deliver groceries, food, and parcels to every corner of the
city (Heipihou 2020). Riders are compared to "everyday heroes of
the times" who "safeguard the economy and people's livelihoods"
(China News, 2020) and warm the hearts of fellow citizens in social
isolation by offering extra "caring service[s]" (M. Yan 2020).

Indeed, it has become a global phenomenon, and rightly so, to
celebrate COVID-19 frontline workers, among whom are health

workers, couriers, and community volunteers. It is also true that
during the pandemic, customers left appreciative reviews and
tips in show of support. (Tipping is not customary in China). Some
600,000 tipping messages were left by customers to Meituan
delivery workers between January 25 and February 24, 2020, with
more than 28,000 mentions of the phrase "take care of yourself"
(Meituan Riders 2020). After all, visibility matters because, as Crain,
Poster, and Cherry note, "work that is not seen is not valued, either
symbolically or materially" (2016, 5).

It is one thing to raise the overdue social and economic recognition of food-delivery riders' labor. However, it is another thing
to capitalize on the moment to foreground a mediated image of
the everyday hero with a keen sense of morality and social duty.
The "responsibilization" (Shamir 2008) of riders' work in platform
capitalism, however, blends the moral order of Chinese family
values with the individualization of the neoliberal regime as to
assuage the rising tensions between the normative imperative of
"new forms of employment" and the intensification of precarity for
the food-delivery workers. In so doing, media representations of
food-delivery workers help depoliticize workers' labor struggles by
displacing them with moral evocations.

A critical piece of information omitted in all Zhixiao Gao's stories is
his employment status. His uniform, which says Meituan Paotui (lit-
erarily meaning to "run errands"), suggests that Gao is most likely a
crowdsourced rider (Figure 1) with minimum levels of institutional
labor protection and collective bargaining power. Meituan Paotui
(launched in 2017) is a TaskRabbit-like platform that crowdsources
the purchase and delivery of errands.

This omission is not accidental. Rather, it indicates that new
meaning-making efforts have entered the fray so that prime food-
delivery riders think of their jobs from the point of view of offering
social and public services. Before 2020, the media depiction of
food-delivery riders mainly focused on their alarming speed on
the road and their lives (including work conditions and labor

management). In late 2016, for example, the image of rushing riders who ignore traffic rules started to enter the public eye. Media outlets like *Xinhua Daily, Beijing Daily,* and *Legal Daily* published stories investigating the factors that force "riders to risk their life for delivery" (Yao 2017). The image of "dangerous riders" or "crazy couriers" reached a climax when Beijing, Shanghai, and other cities announced a spike in the accidents involving food-delivery riders in 2017, with one city having 18 accidents on a daily basis in the first half of 2017 (W. Xiao and Guo 2017). These stories exposed the punitive labor management regime that hinges on timeliness, workers' widespread lack of labor contracts or workplace injury insurance (G. Xu 2017), and their heavy workload and long hours (Z. Li and Xiao 2016). Many urged regulators to hold the platform companies accountable for upholding labor standards and protecting workers' "basic rights" (X. Chen 2017). Others turned to consumers, pleading them to show more compassion and respect before rushing the rider or filing a complaint about a delayed delivery (J. Xu 2017). In November 2019, two months before the coronavirus outbreak, *People's Daily,* arguably the most authoritative media organization in China, compared food-delivery workers to "the creator and guardian of a good life in the city" and called for "more car[e]" from customers, "more support" from the restaurants, and more security from the platform company and social security systems (X. Li 2019). Already here we witness the slow shift of the official framing of these workers, from traffic rule breakers and precarious workers, to viewing them as part of a social support network or privatized social service that accelerates during and post-COVID-19.

From the coverage of the hardship of food-delivery work, a second image of riders emerged that portrayed them as the embodiment of virtues such as hard work, self-sacrifice, and dedication to the family. For example, a feature on three female riders in Beijing highlighted how they endure hardship, support the family, care for the children, the elderly and sick parents, and at the same time, remain optimistic about building a better life from their industri-

ousness (Zhou 2019). The media representation of food-delivery
riders goes beyond the emphasis on family responsibility. Pan
(2019, 13) discovered that Ele.me has reappropriated the concept
of "chivalry spirit," as associated with the gamified knight system of
the riders, with the aim to promote "a social code of conduct" and
"a public collective identity" to govern riders' work performance
and establish the relationship between individual, family, urban
life, and society. Therefore, the job of food-delivery is framed
as fulfilling not only platform-mediated orders but also the civic
and social responsibility for maintaining the urban on-demand
consumer culture. A rider was reported as saying that being an Ele.
me rider is "his way to protect his small family and the big family"
of society (Ele.me 2020).

The efforts to cement the civic and social responsibility of
food-delivery riders to their job are also seen in state media. In
November 2019, Xinhua News Agency published a feature on three
Meituan food-delivery riders from poverty-stricken rural areas,
who, through hard work and fortitude, eventually earned a decent
living in the city, found "meaning" in their (work) life, and fulfilled
their duties as breadwinners and caregivers in the family (Xinhua
Net 2019). The article concluded by claiming that food-delivery
workers are exemplary figures in contemporary Chinese economy:

> Countless honest and modest workers put a wheel
> behind the Chinese economy with their unstoppable
> diligence, laying the foundation for the country to march
> forward. They were not born with a silver spoon in their
> mouth, but their unyielding diligence and self-motivation
> is the witness and epitome of the perseverance of Chi-
> nese economy in prosperity and adversity (Xinhua Net
> 2019).

The media images of riders evolved from showing them as precarious workers who were in need of regulatory intervention for labor
protection to extolling them as workers who submit to neoliberal
responsibility and associate their individual jobs with familial duties

as well as their contributions as citizens to a prosperous Chinese economy.

The creation of the image of the hero laborer or model worker for propaganda purposes has a long history in China (Mees and Zhang 2011; Pugsley 2006), but the heroizing of ordinary food-delivery riders is neither ideologically driven nor propagating the superhuman work ethic as was seen in the socialist tradition. Rather, the stories and constructed images of food-delivery workers have done the cultural work to encode value and moral orientations (Hall 1973) for workers and the public to perceive and evaluate their jobs in the platform economy.

The dominant narrative is that a worker can work flexibly on the platform, lead a self-responsible and self-reliant life in a possibly upward direction, and, in so doing, contribute to a larger cause by serving their country and society, whether this be as the hero during a crisis or as a participant worker helping to develop a future-facing digital platform economy. The dominant narrative also seems to reconcile the individualistic pursuit of autonomy with the call for the collective enterprise of social development. What is brushed aside, however, is the moral and ethical prescription as it weighs on food-delivery workers. Being agile, resourceful, responsible, responsive, and most importantly, raising no questions when the request arrives on the phone, are what is most valorized in flexible capitalism (Sharma 2014) and the current mode of capitalistic accumulation in the platform economy (Chen and Sun 2020).

In September 2020 after China had overcome the health crisis caused by COVID-19 and was enduring the social and economic ramifications of the pandemic, an article published in *Renwu* entitled "Delivery Workers, Trapped in the System" went viral in both thes Chinese and English mediascapes.[10] It offered a meticulous and visceral depiction of riders struggling with platform algorithmic control over on-time delivery. As documented earlier, reporting on the travails of food delivery work per se is not new, but the image of riders "trapped in the system" went viral. The viral circulation of the image of the trapped rider can partly be attributed to the timing—that is, after the pandemic when consumers' appreciation of riders' work was on the rise and the constructed image of the delivery hero was widespread. The article did not elaborate on the labor management aspect of platforms, mentioning labor rights and the need for regulation in passing, but it triggered public outcry against the platforms. Ele.me immediately announced a new button on the app interface for the customers to indicate if they "are willing to wait for 5/10 more minutes." The action backfired quickly, and Ele.me was criticized for shifting the responsibility to customers. Meituan announced a series of technological optimization measures and promised to improve the rewards system for riders with good performance.

It remains to be seen whether the viral images of food-delivery worker being trapped in the system and being the ordinary hero will lead to substantive changes in labor protection or further regulations of the platform economy. But 2020 and the post-pandemic period could be a crisis-induced moment for social and economic change. Nevertheless, if the change remains at the level of technological solutions or the reliance on consumers' compassion, the media spotlight that portrays riders as everyday heroes would at best be a symbolic reward in exchange for deferred improvements to work conditions and persistent social inequalities. The positive and uplifting images of the self-reliant, responsible, and enduring rider may have simply become powerful mediation tools to depoliticize labor struggles by shifting this work to moral grounds, while leaving intact the capitalistic logic and management technique underlying the "trapping" system.

‖‖‖‖‖‖‖‖‖‖‖‖‖‖

The chapter uses spaces of mediation as an analytical angle and heuristic device to comprehend the multifaceted interplay between media and management in structuring the labor process and shaping the "common sense" about the requirements and expectations of working in the platform economy in China. This approach is in line with existing research that addresses the (re-)territorialization of workforce management made possible by capitalism, technology, management thinking, and organizational restructuring (Peck and Theodore 2001; Tsing 2009; Cowen 2014). It also corresponds to media scholars' realization that media needs to be problematized, as Zehle and Rossiter put it, not merely "in terms of communication systems, but as a constellation that organizes the production of life and labor" (2015).

Going "in search for media"—as this book series is called—requires recognizing the possibility and perhaps inevitability of the fluid composition of technology, organization, market, and knowledge morphing into the terms of media that condition our lives. However, to avoid relativism and media determinism, it is crucial to pinpoint the social actors—including both workers and managers— and to untangle their respective and combined mobilization of technology, discourse, and management practices to achieve certain models of mediation. Concerning labor management, this means tracing the multiple and flexible organizational shapes that materialize labor management practices. As this chapter shows, platform-mediated labor management involves assembling, disassembling, and reassembling the work force. But the dynamic management of the platform does not exist in the technological wonder of algorithms or big data alone. It is achieved through exploiting the existing labor intermediary industry, lagging regulation, and an aspiring central government that regards digital technology as the primary driving force for economic and social development and hence proactively shapes the public understanding of the platform work.

Therefore, studying the meditations of labor points to distinct layers and scopes of management practice and technology, which offer valuable entry points to confront the current terrain of labor politics. Above all, this entails an expanded understanding of media and management technologies. The study of labor management must focus on the practice and technology of management as deployed through temp staffing agencies and platforms at the workplace or in the labor process. It must also investigate the

production, circulation, and rearticulation of management ideas as
they are mediated by the environment and consumed by society;
this includes attention to the space of mass media, the domain
of government policy, and knowledge-production entities like
universities. My intervention here has hence been twofold: First,
to foreground the relevance of policy to management and media
studies, particularly regarding its role in shaping commonly held
beliefs about certain social and cultural phenomena. Though
studying the government's role is a stable and perhaps unavoid-
able subject whenever the research is concerned with China, the
cultural roles played by the policy or regulatory documents are
worth exploring in other countries, too. My second intervention
is to bridge research subjects in management studies and media
studies—namely the labor process and the analysis of media representations, respectively. Bridging these domains potentially opens
a viable path to exploring the connections between the formation
of worker subjectivity, management practices in the labor process,
and management as enacted by the state.

Among the transformations that have happened to the world of
work, one of the most astonishing is the hegemonic trope of non-
work (Tsing 2009), which ranges from self-exploitation in the name
of aspiration (Duffy 2016), to transnational cultural currency given
to the figure of the entrepreneur (Irani 2019), to the social service
provided by food-delivery workers during COVID-19 as demonstrated in this chapter. Meaning making and common sense–shaping are
of great significance for workers' subjective and labor politics, and
to examine them, scholars have to broaden the lens of focus from
platforms themselves to the regulatory, institutional, and media
representations through which labor is mediated and managed.
There is a growing body of work on worker activism and resistance
in the platform economy, but few on their struggles, as well as
victories, of being represented on the policy agenda and even less
on workers' alternative cultural production to challenge normative
narratives about the platform work. The management spaces of
labor mediation should also be the spaces of labor politics.

Notes

1 A handful of recent research on the experience in different geographies is found in two special journal issues (Kloet et al. 2019; Steinberg and Li 2017).

2 A work unit (or *danwei* in Chinese) is a formal organization in socialist China that principally rests on one's employment relation. It is also the social unit for collective civil life and socialist welfare programs (e.g. childcare).

3 The term "slashie youth" was apparently inspired by Alboher (2007), but no reference was offered in Ele.me's report.

4 Interviews were conducted in 2018, and the names used in the chapter are pseudonyms.

5 Chinese food delivery platforms commonly adopt a gamified hierarchical Knight system for riders, wherein a rider's ranking corresponds to the piece rate pay one may get (see Sun 2019). Riders are sometimes called knight, which is also a wordplay, as "Knight" (骑士) shares the first Chinese character with "rider" (骑手).

6 Ele.me was founded in 2009, Meituan in 2013, and Baidu Waimai in 2014. They were the three largest market players until August 2017 when Ele.me purchased Baidu Waimai.

7 The median monthly wage in Beijing in 2017 was $983.

8 Thanks to Ping Sun for this information.

9 All quotes from Gao in this paragraph were from the video interview posted on the *Time* website. Author's translation.

10 The article's English version is available at: http://chuangcn.org/2020/11/delivery-renwu-translation/.

References

Alboher, Marci. 2007. One Person / Multiple Careers: A New Model for Work/Life Success. New York: Business Plus.

Allon, Gad, Maxime Cohen, and Park Sinchaisri. 2018. "The Impact of Behavioral and Economic Drivers on Gig Economy Workers." SSRN Scholarly Paper ID 3274628. Rochester, N.Y.: Social Science Research Network. https://papers.ssrn.com/abstract=3274628.

Andrijasevic, Rutvica, and Devi Sacchetto. 2017. "'Disappearing Workers': Foxconn in Europe and the Changing Role of Temporary Work Agencies:" *Work, Employment and Society,* 31, no. 1: 54–70. https://doi.org/10.1177/0950017015622918.

Boltanski, Luc, and Eve Chiapello. 2007. *The New Spirit of Capitalism.* Trans. Gregory Elliott. London: Verso.

Çalışkan, Koray, and Michel Callon. 2010. "Economization, Part 2: A Research Programme for the Study of Markets." *Economy and Society* 39, no. 1: 1–32. https://doi.org/10.1080/03085140903424519.

Campbell, Charlie. 2020. "These Delivery Drivers Are Risking Their Health to Keep China Running during the Coronavirus Epidemic." *Time.* March 16, 2020. https://time.com/5803803/china-delivery-driver-ecommerce-covid19/.

Chen, Julie Yujie. 2018. "Thrown under the Bus and Outrunning It! The Logic of DiDi and Taxi Drivers' Labour and Activism in the On-Demand Economy." *New Media & Society* 20, no. 8: 2691–711. https://doi.org/10.1177/1461444817729149.

Chen, Julie Yujie. 2020. "The Mirage and Politics of Participation in China's Platform Economy." *Javnost—The Public* 27, no. 2: 154–70. https://doi.org/10.1080/13183222 .2020.1727271.

Chen, Julie Yujie, and Ping Sun. 2020. "Temporal Arbitrage, the Fragmented Rush, and Opportunistic Behaviors: The Labor Politics of Time in the Platform Economy." *New Media & Society* 22, no. 9: 1561–79. https://doi.org/10.1177/1461444820913567.

Chen, Xiaoyan. 2017. "What Drives Riders to Rush Crazily?" *Workers Daily*, October 15, 2017.

China News. 2020. "The New Opportunities for the Food-Delivery Industry Brought by the Outbreak of the Coronavirus." *China News.* April 6, 2020. http://www.china news.com/cj/2020/04-06/9148613.shtml.

Couldry, Nick, and Andreas Hepp. 2016. *The Mediated Construction of Reality.* Cambridge, UK: Polity.

Cowen, Deborah. 2016. *The Deadly Life of Logistics: Mapping Violence in Global Trade.* Minneapolis: University of Minnesota Press.

Crain, Marion G., Winifred Poster, and Miriam A. Cherry, eds. 2016. *Invisible Labor: Hidden Work in the Contemporary World.* Oakland: University of California Press.

DiDi Institute of Policy Study. 2017. "New Economy, New Jobs: 2017 Research Report on Jobs on DiDi Chuxing." Beijing, China: DiDi Institute of Policy Study.

Dijck, Jose van, Thomas Poell, and Martijn de Waal. 2018. *The Platform Society.* New York: Oxford University Press.

Duffy, Brooke Erin. 2016. "The Romance of Work: Gender and Aspirational Labour in the Digital Culture Industries." *International Journal of Cultural Studies* 19, no. 4: 441–57. https://doi.org/10.1177/1367877915572186.

Ele.me. 2020. "2020 Ele.me Blue Knight Research Report." Shanghai. https://www .sohu.com/a/390207782_384789.

Gawer, Annabelle, ed. 2011. *Platforms, Markets, and Innovation.* Cheltenham, UK: Edward Elgar Publishers.

Gregg, Melissa. 2011. *Work's Intimacy.* London: Polity.

Gregg, Melissa. 2018. *Counterproductive: Time Management in the Knowledge Economy.* Durham, N.C.: Duke University Press.

Hall, Stuart. 1973. "Encoding and Decoding in the Television Discourse." Birmingham, UK. http://epapers.bham.ac.uk/2962/1/Hall,_1973,_Encoding_and_Decoding_in_ the_Television_Discourse.pdf.

Heipihou. 2020. "The Chinese Face on the *Time Magazine* Cover: How Did This Food-Delivery Rider Reach the Peak of His Life?" *The Paper.* April 1, 2020. https://m.the paper.cn/baijiahao_6775962.

Hong, Yu. 2017. *Networking China: The Digital Transformation of the Chinese Economy.* Urbana: University of Illinois Press.

Hou, Rui. 2019. "The Commercialisation of Internet-Opinion Management: How the Market Is Engaged in State Control in China." *New Media & Society,* November. https://doi.org/10.1177/1461444819889959.

Hyman, Louis. 2018. *Temp: How American Work, American Business, and the American Dream Became Temporary.* New York: Viking.

Irani, Lilly. 2015. "Difference and Dependence among Digital Workers: The Case of Amazon Mechanical Turk." *South Atlantic Quarterly* 114, no. 1: 225–34. https://doi .org/10.1215/00382876-2831665.

Irani, Lilly. 2019. *Chasing Innovation: Making Entrepreneurial Citizens in Modern India.* Princeton, N.J.: Princeton University Press.

Kenney, Martin, and John Zysman. 2016. "The Rise of the Platform Economy." *Issues in Science and Technology,* Spring. http://issues.org/32-3/the-rise-of-the-platform -economy/.

Kloet, Jeroen de, Thomas Poell, Guohua Zeng, and Yiu Fai Chow. 2019. "The Platformization of Chinese Society. Infrastructure, Governance, and Practice." *Chinese Journal of Communication* 12, no. 3: 249–56. https://doi.org/10.1080/17544750.20 19.1644008.

Langley, Paul, and Andrew Leyshon. 2017. "Platform Capitalism: The Intermediation and Capitalization of Digital Economic Circulation." *Finance and Society* 3, no. 1: 11–31. https://doi.org/10.2218/finsoc.v3i1.1936.

Lee, Ching Kwan, and Yelizavetta Kofman. 2012. "The Politics of Precarity: Views beyond the United States." *Work and Occupations* 39, no. 4: 388–408. https://doi .org/10.1177/0730888412446710.

Li, Xinping. 2019. "What Can We Do for the Food-Delivery Workers?" *People's Daily,* November 29.

Li, Ze, and Peng Xiao. 2016. "The Predicament behind the High-Income of Food-Delivery." *Beijing Business Today,* May 11.

Liu, Xiao. 2019. *Information Fantasies: Precarious Mediation in Postsocialist China.* Minneapolis: University of Minnesota Press.

Mees, B., and J. Zhang. 2011. "Chinese Worker Heroes: Between Patriotism and Nostalgia." In *Challenges for International Business in a Turbulent Global Environment,* 1–7. Melbourne: Australia and New Zealand International Business Academy. https://researchbank.rmit.edu.au/view/rmit:15757.

Meituan Dianping. 2018. "2018 Research Report on Food-Delivery Riders." May 4. http://www.199it.com/archives/720183.html.

Meituan Riders. 2020. "Meituan Rider on the Cover of TIME, the Only Chinese Face in a Global Snapshot of Fighting against the Coronavirus!" March 19. https://mp .weixin.qq.com/s/QR7HjH9tnNagdqKl_1GEXQ.

Mezzadra, Sandro, and Brett Neilson. 2013. *Border as Method, or, The Multiplication of Labor.* Durham, N.C.: Duke University Press.

Moore, James. 1993. "Predators and Prey: A New Ecology of Competition." *Harvard Business Review,* May 1. https://hbr.org/1993/05/predators-and-prey-a-new -ecology-of-competition.

Moore, Phoebe, and Simon Joyce. 2019. "Black Box or Hidden Abode? The Expansion and Exposure of Platform Work Managerialism." *Review of International Political Economy* 27, no. 4: 926–48. https://doi.org/10.1080/09692290.2019.1627569.

Pan, Weixian. 2019. "China Southern: Digital Environments as Geopolitical Contact Zones." PhD Diss., Montréal, Canada: Concordia University.

Peck, Jamie, and Nik Theodore. 2001. "Contingent Chicago: Restructuring the Spaces of Temporary Labor." *International Journal of Urban and Regional Research* 25, no. 3: 471–96. https://doi.org/10.1111/1468-2427.00325.

People's Daily. 2018. "Internet+: Activating New Forms of Work." March 17. http://www.gov.cn/xinwen/2018-03/17/content_5274880.htm.

Pugsley, Peter C. 2006. "Constructing the Hero: Nationalistic News Narratives in Contemporary China." *Westminster Papers in Communication and Culture* 3, no. 1: 78. https://doi.org/10.16997/wpcc.17.

Rochet, Jean-Charles, and Jean Tirole. 2003. "Platform Competition in Two-Sided Markets." *Journal of the European Economic Association* 1, no. 4: 990–1029. https://doi.org/10.1162/154247603322493212.

Rosenblat, Alex, and Luke Stark. 2016. "Algorithmic Labor and Information Asymmetries: A Case Study of Uber's Drivers." *International Journal of Communication* 10 (July): 3758–84.

Schneider, Florian. 2018. *China's Digital Nationalism.* New York: Oxford University Press.

Shamir, Ronen. 2008. "The Age of Responsibilization: On Market-Embedded Morality." *Economy and Society* 37, no. 1: 1–19. https://doi.org/10.1080/03085140701760833.

Sharma, Sarah. 2014. *In the Meantime: Temporality and Cultural Politics.* Durham, N.C.: Duke University Press.

Shatil, Sharron. 2020. "Managerialism—A Social Order on the Rise." *Critical Sociology,* March. https://doi.org/10.1177/0896920520911703.

State Council. 2017. "Opinions of the State Council on Effectively Ensuring Employment and Entrepreneurship at Current and Future Periods." April 13. http://www.gov.cn/zhengce/content/2017-04/19/content_5187179.htm.

Steinberg, Marc. 2019. *The Platform Economy: How Japan Transformed the Consumer Internet.* Minneapolis: University of Minnesota Press.

Steinberg, Marc, and Jinying Li. 2017. "Introduction: Regional Platforms." *Asiascape: Digital Asia* 4, no. 3: 173–83. https://doi.org/10.1163/22142312-12340076.

Sun, Ping. 2019. "Your Order, Their Labor: An Exploration of Algorithms and Laboring on Food Delivery Platforms in China." *Chinese Journal of Communication* 12, no. 3: 308–23. https://doi.org/10.1080/17544750.2019.1583676.

Time Staff. 2020. "Behind the Covers of TIME's Special Coronavirus Issue." *Time.* March 19. https://time.com/5805947/time-coronavirus-covers/.

Thomas, Llewellyn D. W., Erkko Autio, and David M. Gann. 2014. "Architectural Leverage: Putting Platforms in Context." *Academy of Management Perspectives* 28, no. 2: 198–219. https://doi.org/10.5465/amp.2011.0105.

Tsing, Anna. 2009. "Supply Chains and the Human Condition." *Rethinking Marxism* 21, no. 2: 148–76. https://doi.org/10.1080/08935690902743088.

Wang, Jing. 2001. "The State Question in Chinese Popular Cultural Studies." *Inter-Asia Cultural Studies* 2, no. 1: 35–52. https://doi.org/10.1080/14649370120039443.

Wen, Xiaoyi. 2018. "The Nature of Sharing Economy Is Labor-Intensive Economy." *The Paper.* December 10. https://www.thepaper.cn/newsDetail_forward_2716522.

Xiao, Gang. 2019. "Accelerating the Establishment of the Framework and System for

the New Forms of Employment." *Guangmingwang.* October 15. http://www.gmw
.cn/xueshu/2019-10/15/content_33233631.htm.

Xiao, Wei, and Shihui Guo. 2017. "Food-Delivery: Imbalance between Efficiency and
Morality." *Beijing Business Today,* September 15.

Xinhua Net. 2019. "The Resilience of China's Economy: Meituan Riders Hold Up."
Xinhua Net. November 12. http://www.xinhuanet.com/tech/2019-11/12/c_1125
220606.htm.

Xinhua News Agency. 2015. "The Bulletin of the Communist Party of China in the Fifth
Plenary Session of the 18th CPC Central Committee." Xinhua Net. October 29.
http://www.xinhuanet.com//politics/2015-10/29/c_1116983078.htm.

Xu, Feng. 2013. "Temporary Work in China Precarity in an Emerging Labour Market."
In *Temporary Work, Agencies and Unfree Labour : Insecurity in the New World of
Work,* ed. Judy Fudge and Kendra Strauss, 143–63. London: Routledge. https://doi
.org/10.4324/9780203111390.

Xu, Guanying. 2017. "Lightening Speed to Deliver Convenience." *Xinhua Daily,* March 28.

Xu, Jinghui. 2017. "When They Are Busy under the Blazing Sun." *Wenhui Bao,* July 18.

Yan, Hairong. 2003. "Neoliberal Governmentality and Neohumanism: Organizing
Suzhi/Value Flow through Labor Recruitment Networks." *Cultural Anthropology* 18,
no. 4: 493–523. https://doi.org/10.1525/can.2003.18.4.493.

Yan, Mi. 2020. "Thumbs Up! Food-Delivery Rider's Caring Service Is Heartwarming."
International Business Daily, April 17.

Yao, Xing. 2017. "Who Ask Riders to Exchange Their Life for Food-Delivery." *Beijing
Daily,* September 1.

Zehle, Soenke, and Ned Rossiter. 2015. "Mediations of Labor: Algorithmic Archi-
tectures, Logistical Media, and the Rise of Black Box Politics." January 5. https://
nedrossiter.org/?p=453.

Zhang, Chenggang. 2019. *Employment Transformation: Digital Business Models and New
Forms of Employment in China*. Beijing: China Workers Publishing House.

Zhao, Yuezhi. 2003. "Transnational Capital, the Chinese State, and China's Communication Industries in a Fractured Society." *Javnost—The Public* 10, no. 4: 53–74.
https://doi.org/10.1080/13183222.2003.11008841.

Zhou, Yi. 2019. "The Life of Three Female Riders in Beijing." *Workers Daily,* February 28.

Closures and Openings

Rutvica Andrijasevic, Julie Yujie Chen, Melissa Gregg, and Marc Steinberg

As we were writing this book, empty supermarket shelves and a dearth of personal protective equipment served as deadly warnings of just-in-time inventory supply and its failures. Citizens the world over came to appreciate the interdependence of nations, the porosity of borders, and the complexity of defining some work as more "essential" than others. The spreading coronavirus intensified nationalist sentiment already promulgated by then-President Donald Trump (among others), seeking reelection in the United States, with China-bashing and anti-Asian racism and violence on the rise in North America and beyond. Against recent trends, manufacturing of everything from hand sanitizer to vaccines came to resemble a national contest, as populism and paranoia fueled calls for the reshoring of production facilities.

COVID-19 tested many of the original conditions bringing the idea of this book together—conference networks dependent on cheap air travel, the prospect of in-person collaboration, even predictable time frames and locations for writing. Meeting, connecting, and workshopping remotely across time zones via Skype, this book is a COVID bubble of its own, a venue to collectively process the transformations we have been living through. It was hard to ignore the stark contrasts in employee experience as remote work suddenly became the norm, and Zoom entered our daily vocabulary replacing classrooms. In manufacturing companies from Foxconn in Europe to Intel in Oregon, the ability of knowledge workers to retreat to the safety of home offices clashed with the need for fab workers to guard assembly lines stretched to meet the increased demand for computers and home electronics.

The mandate to stay at home offered a chance for us to witness the changing media environment at the heart of the platform economy today, as Netflix and food delivery became a common means by which to *pass the time* that lockdown required. On-demand services sustained the appetites of consumers in cities across the globe, revealing a vast logistics infrastructure that felt more reliable than government or welfare. How Amazon's brand surged as both a service provider and employer throughout the 2020 pandemic is another lesson in platform economics, as it began presenting itself as the new Red Cross (Lee and Nilsson 2020). Like Netflix, Amazon Prime capitalizes on the temporal acceleration of logistics fulfilment, setting the standard for "same day" delivery. The popularity of over-the-top streaming services, along with other sectors that rely on the infrastructures of the internet and cloud computing, in turn stimulates a boom in the manufacturing of hardware, including chips, servers, storage, cables, and so on. In the meantime, the placement of private content-delivery networks (e.g. Netflix's Open Connect) in geographically strategic locations that are proximate to the targeted audience is motivated by the "time-based competition" in content delivery (Lobato 2019), recalling the real-time mandates of production Andrijasevic documents here, albeit in consumer-facing form.

The temporal immediacy and convenience of video on demand has been a theme running throughout accounts of video-streaming platforms from Netflix to AbemaTV to Tudou (Lotz 2017; Lobato 2019; Li 2019; Appadurai and Alexander 2020). Overlooked in these discussions is the earlier model of production outlined in this book that subtends the on-demand logics of internet-distributed video: just-in-time (JIT). JIT's model of manufacture and circulation presumes the "on-demand" delivery of parts to the factory and products to the consumer with impacts on supply-chain management, software development, labor practices, and more. Further reflection on the parallels and distinctions between JIT and on-demand platforms will deepen our understanding of the politics of on-demand streaming services and the manufacturing histories that underlie them. This work will also raise awareness of the labor practices both of these presume. How are emerging logistical models of film production, or what Kay Dickinson has called "supply chain cinema" (Dickinson 2016; 2020), tied in with on-demand streaming? How does "platform television" (Crawford 2021) transpose the temporalities and "efficiencies" of no-waste and on-time delivery from production to consumption and back to production again?

Netflix CEO Reed Hastings has promoted his company's embrace of management "on the edge of chaos" (recalling management guru Tom Peters's 1987 bestseller, *Thriving on Chaos*) and noted the difference between managing a creative industry and managing a factory (Peters 1987; Ryssdal and Hollenhorst 2020). And yet, the creative industry *is* a site of the industrialized production of audio-visual material, one whose production techniques operate through what industry studies scholar John Caldwell calls "stress aesthetics" (Caldwell 2013)—a model not so far removed from the description of Toyotism as "management by stress" (Parker and Slaughter 1988). As video-streaming services have seen subscriber numbers skyrocket during COVID-19, and film theaters have shuttered or faced bankruptcy, bringing discussions of Toyotism and JIT to bear on articulations of on-demand streaming platforms offers a topical site for ongoing study.

The geopolitics of information technology between China and the United States will also cast a long shadow over the management of media in the next decade. In 2020, right-wing conspiracies blamed 5G and China for the production of the coronavirus and its subsequent global contagion. Meanwhile then-U.S. President Donald Trump's insistent reference to the "Wuhan virus" or "China virus" to describe COVID-19 doubtless contributed to a growth in anti-Asian

racism and hate crimes in North America. This anti-China posture
continues post-Trump as well. Returning to the hardware histories
discussed in this book, American China-bashing in the present
bears remarkable similarities to the anxieties centered on Japan in
the 1980s. A combination of xenophobia, techno-nationalism, and
Orientalism (Ueno 1999; Morley and Robins 1995) mix with claims
to white supremacy, data sovereignty, national security, and the
right to manufacture technologies, culminating in the arrogant
belief of world leadership in intellectual property. The dangers
supposedly posed by China in the wake of COVID-19 unfortunately
recall "yellow peril" discourses deployed to dehumanize Asians
migrants in the nineteenth century and the Japanese during
World War II.

The rise of anti-Chinese racism in the United States, notes Joshua
Neves, foregrounds "the inequality of global supply chains—a
current logic of racialized capitalism—which seek to move things
in specific directions and keep everyone in their place" (Neves
2020). The bogeyman of China has loomed particularly large since
the Trump presidency, which itself was as much a symptom as a
cause of geopolitical tensions. Indeed, Trump's public campaign
against China mirrors his anti-Japanese rants of the 1980s (which,
again, were symptomatic of the Japan-bashing times). "There is
going to be a tremendous backlash against what Japan is doing in
this country," Trump said in 1988, "sucking the lifeblood out of it
because of our stupid policies. Our policy is to have free trade, but
Japan is not reciprocating" (Easton 1988). Trump's rhetoric and the
surge in anti-Asian hate crimes during COVID reflect deep-seated
racial bias against Asians, as well as fears about the place of China
in the contemporary world system: "Contagion thus not only refers
to the unruliness of new flu strains, but to the new mobilities of
Chinese people, products, and technologies" (Neves 2020).

And yet, the current moment is different when one takes the politics of 5G communications networks to the level of infrastructure.
The American ban on Huawei and its pressures on American allies
to follow suit since 2018 surface American tech policy's fixation on

national security (W. Chen 2019) and China's decades-long struggle
with a heavy dependence on foreign proprietary technologies and
transnational corporations. China's pursuit of so-called indigenous
(read: national) technological development (Zhao 2010) makes
visible how the discourses of national innovation and "network
sovereignty" are inscribing a distinctive techno-nationalistic mark
on Chinese tech firms and Chinese technology. This has resulted in
continued competition and contestation between the United States
and China in shaping contemporary and future global technological
terrains, from internet governance and technological development
to 5G infrastructure and standards (Tang 2020; Zhao 2010). As
we have argued throughout this book, hardware is the site of
competing sovereignties, where management means controlling
not only the technologies themselves but also the imagined futures
that they represent. Like Cold War competition and the Toyotism
anxiety that succeeded it, management involves mediating percep-
tions of national eminence and the belief that one nation will have
control over the economic order to come.

This final concern over competing futurities may point to alternative ways of assessing and constructing media theory. Following
Kuan-Hsing Chen's (2010) provocation to use "Asia as method" to
undo the imperialist imaginary, the question we bring to this book
series is: What is the role of Asia in the production and orientation
of media theory and media studies? And how, in turn, might inter-
Asian solidarities mitigate against the nationalist competition over
control of the future to come? For instance, what model of capitalism is needed if we agree that one of the largest e-commerce
companies in the world—Alibaba—operates not as a paradigm
of "platform capitalism," as Srnicek would have it, but rather, as
Lin Zhang (2020) puts it, as "petty capitalism," a unique form of
"small-scale and family-based flexible regimes of production in
China"? Or if the bazaar and the emporium were the real models of
the platform marketplaces at work today, as per Adrian Athique's
(2019) analysis of platforms in India?

In this regard, our book aims to unsettle the orthodox flows of knowledge in media and management theory from the North Atlantic to the Asia Pacific. We channel theories and manufacturing histories from East Asia in order to show their relevance to the way "we" think, write, and make a living on devices. The knowledge we have uncovered around hardware manufacturing in the Asia Pacific is a crucial part of—and sometimes counterpoint to—the stories told about media and its management in Europe and North America.

References

Appadurai, Arjun, and Neta Alexander. 2020. *Failure.* Cambridge: Polity Press Medford.

Athique, Adrian. 2019. "Digital Emporiums: Platform Capitalism in India," *Media Industries Journal* 6, no. 2. https://doi.org/10.3998/mij.15031809.0006.205.

Caldwell, John T. 2013. "Stress Aesthetics and Deprivation Payroll Systems." In *Behind the Screen: Inside European Production Cultures,* ed. Petr Szczepanik and Patrick Vonderau, 91–111. New York: Palgrave Macmillan US. https://doi.org/10.1057/978 1137282187_7.

Chen, Kuan-Hsing. 2010. *Asia as Method: Toward Deimperialization.* Durham, N.C.: Duke University Press

Chen, Wenhong. 2019. "Now I Know My ABCs: U.S–China Policy on AI, Big Data, and Cloud Computing. *Asia-Pacific Issues* 140 (September). https://www.eastwest center.org/publications/now-i-know-my-abcs-us-china-policy-ai-big-data-and -cloud-computing.

Crawford, Colin Jon Mark. 2021. *Netflix's Speculative Fictions: Financializing Platform Television.* Lanham: Lexington Books.

Dickinson, Kay. 2016. *Arab Cinema Travels: Transnational Syria, Palestine, Dubai, and Beyond.* London: Macmillan International Higher Education.

———. 2020. "'Make It What You Want It to Be': Logistics, Labor, and Land Financialization via the Globalized Free Zone Studio." In *In the Studio: Visual Creation and Its Material Environments,* ed. Brian Jacobson. Berkeley: University of California Press.

Easton, Nina. 1988. "Now, Mr. Trump, What About L.A.?" *Los Angeles Times,* July 24, 1988. https://www.latimes.com/archives/la-xpm-1988-07-24-tm-10040-story.html.

Lee, Dave, and Patricia Nilsson. 2020. "Amazon Auditions to Be 'The New Red Cross' in Covid-19 Crisis." *Financial Times,* March 31, 2020. https://www.ft.com/content/220bf850-726c-11ea-ad98-044200cb277f.

Li, Luzhou. 2019. *Zoning China : Online Video, Popular Culture, and the State.* Information Policy Series. Cambridge: The MIT Press. https://ieeexplore.ieee.org/servlet/opac?bknumber=8925388.

Lobato, R. 2019. *Netflix Nations: The Geography of Digital Distribution.* New York: New York University Press.

Lotz, Amanda D. 2017. *Portals: A Treatise on Internet-Distributed Television.* Ann Arbor: Michigan Publishing, University of Michigan Library.

Morley, David, and Kevin Robins. 1995. "Techno-Orientalism: Japan Panic." In *Spaces of Identity: Global Media, Electronic Landscapes, and Cultural Boundaries,* 147–73. London: Routledge.

Neves, Joshua. 2020. "The Coronavirus (COVID-19), Anti-Chinese Racism, and the Politics of Underglobalization." Durham, N.C.: Duke University Press News. 2020. https://dukeupress.wordpress.com/2020/03/11/joshua-neves-on-the-corona virus-covid-19-anti-chinese-racism-and-the-politics-of-underglobalization/.

Parker, Mike, and Jane Slaughter. 1988. "Management by Stress." *Technology Review* 91, no. 7: 37–44.

Peters, Thomas J. 1987. *Thriving on Chaos: Handbook for a Management Revolution.* New York: Knopf.

Ryssdal, Kai, and Maria Hollenhorst. 2020. "Netflix CEO on Culture, Competition, and What Keeps Him Up at Night." *Marketplace* (blog). September 8, 2020. https://www .marketplace.org/2020/09/08/netflix-ceo-reed-hastings-on-culture-competition -and-what-keeps-him-up-at-night/.

Tang, Min. 2020. "Huawei versus the United States? The Geopolitics of Extraterritorial Internet Infrastructure." *International Journal of Communication* 14: 4556–77.

Ueno, Toshiya. 1999. "Techno-Orientalism and Media-Tribalism: On Japanese Anima-tion and Rave Culture." *Third Text* 13, no. 47: 95–106.

Zhang, Lin. 2020. "When Platform Capitalism Meets Petty Capitalism in China: Alibaba and an Integrated Approach to Platformization." *International Journal of Communi-cation* 14: 114–34.

Zhao, Yuezhi. 2010. "China's Pursuits of Indigenous Innovations in Information Tech-nology Developments: Hopes, Follies, and Uncertainties." *Chinese Journal of Com-munication* 3, no. 3: 266–89. https://doi.org/10.1080/17544`750.2010.499628.

Authors

Rutvica Andrijasevic is associate professor of international migration and business in the School of Management at the University of Bristol. She is author of *Migration, Agency, and Citizenship in Sex Trafficking.*

Julie Yujie Chen is assistant professor in the Institute of Communication, Culture, Information, and Technology (ICCIT) at the University of Toronto Mississauga and holds a graduate appointment in the Faculty of Information. She is lead author of *Super-sticky WeChat and Chinese Society.*

Melissa Gregg is senior principal engineer in the Client Computing Group at Intel. Her previous books include *Counterproductive: Time Management in the Knowledge Economy, Work's Intimacy,* and *The Affect Theory Reader.*

Marc Steinberg is associate professor of film studies at Concordia University. He is the author of *Anime's Media Mix: Franchising Toys and Characters in Japan* (Minnesota, 2012) and *The Platform Economy: How Japan Transformed the Consumer Internet* (Minnesota, 2019).